FOR YOUR OWN PEOPLE
Aelred of Rievaulx's *Pastoral Prayer*

FOR YOUR OWN PEOPLE

AELRED OF RIEVAULX'S
PASTORAL PRAYER

Critical Edition, Introduction,
and Annotations
by
Marsha L. Dutton

Translation
by
Mark DelCogliano

CISTERCIAN PUBLICATIONS
Kalamazoo, Michigan

The edition of Cambridge MS Jesus College Q.B. 17 ff. 97–99 is printed by permission of the Master and Fellows of Jesus College, Cambridge.

The translation, here somewhat amended, previously appeared in *Cistercian Studies Quarterly* 37:4 (2002) 461–466.

*The work of Cistercian Publications
is made possible in part by support from
Western Michigan University
to the Institute of Cistercian Studies.*

Library of Congress Cataloguing-in-Publication Data

Aelred, of Rievaulx, Saint, 1110–1167.
  [Oratio pastoralis. English]
  For your own people : Aelred of Rievaulx's pastoral prayer : critical edition / introduction and annotations by Marsha L. Dutton ; translation by Mark DelCogliano.
    p. cm. — (Cistercian fathers series ; no. 73)
  Includes bibliographical references (p.   ) and indexes.
  ISBN 978-0-87907-273-5
  1. Prayers, Medieval.   I. Dutton, Marsha L.   II. DelCogliano, Mark.
III. Title.   IV. Series.

  BV237.A3613 2008
  264'.13—dc22   2007047564

Printed in the United States of America.

In thanksgiving for the life and gifts of
Father Charles Dumont, OCSO
monk, poet, scholar, shepherd

Table of Contents

List of Abbreviations   ix

Aelred and his Prayer:
  An Introduction to Aelred's *Pastoral Prayer*   1

Oratio Pastoralis
The Pastoral Prayer   37

Select Bibliography   59
Table of Scriptural References   66
Table of Non-Scriptural References   68

List of Abbreviations

GENERAL ABBREVIATIONS

add.	added
cf.	compare
del.	deleted
Div.	Diversi
ed./ed(s).	edited by/editor(s)
Ep(p)	*Epistol(e)*, Letter(s)
in marg.	in the margin
intro.	introduction by
l(l).	line(s)
Med	Meditation
MS(S)	manuscript(s)
n(n).	note(s)
n.d.	no date given
n.p.	no publisher given
OCSO	Cistercian Order [of the Strict Observance]
om.	omitted

Prol	Prologue
rpt.	reprint
S(s)	Sermo(nes), sermon(s)
sup. lin.	above the line
trans.	translated by/translator/translation
UK	United Kingdom
Vlg	Vulgate
vol(s).	volume(s)

FREQUENTLY CITED WORKS

Fry	*RB 1980:The Rule of St. Benedict in Latin and English with Notes.* Ed. Timothy Fry. Collegeville: The Liturgical Press, 1981.
Oratio	Marsha L. Dutton. 'Aelred of Rievaulx's *Oratio* Pastoralis: A New Critical Edition'. CSQ 38 (2003) 297–308.
Peifer	Claude Peifer. 'Appendix 2. The Abbot'. *RB 1980.* Ed. Timothy Fry. Collegeville: The Liturgical Press, 1981. 322–378.
Vita A	*Vita Aelredi.* Ed., trans., and Intro. Maurice Powicke. Oxford: Clarendon, 1950. Trans. rpt: *The Life of Aelred of Rievaulx and the Letter to Maurice.* Intro. Marsha L. Dutton. CF 57. Kalamazoo: Cistercian Publications, 1994.

PERIODICALS AND SERIES

ABR	*American Benedictine Review*
CC	Corpus Christianorum. Turnhout: Brepols Publishers

CCCM	Corpus Christianorum, Continuatio Mediaevalis. Turnhout: Brepols Publishers
CF	Cistercian Fathers series. Spencer, Washington DC, Kalamazoo, 1970–
Cîteaux	*Cîteaux: Commentarii cistercienses; Cîteaux in de Nederlanden.* Westmalle, Belgium; Nuits-Saints-Georges, France; Nazareth, Belgium, 1950–
Coll	*Collectanea cisterciensia; Collectanea o.c.r.*
CS	Cistercian Studies series. Spencer, Washington DC, Kalamazoo, 1969–
CSEL	Corpus Scriptorum Ecclesiasticorum Latinorum
CSQ	*Cistercian Studies / Cistercian Studies Quarterly*
PL	Patrologia cursus completus, series latina. Ed. J.-P. Migne. 221 vols. Paris, 1844–1864
RB	*Regula monachorum Sancti Benedicti, Rule of Saint Benedict*
RBen	*Révue bénédictine.* Maredesous, Belgium, 1884–
SBOp	*Sancti Bernardi Opera.* Ed. J. Leclercq, H. M. Rochais, C. H. Talbot. 8 vols. Rome: Editiones Cistercienses, 1957–1977
SCh	Sources chrétiennes series. Paris: Éditions du Cerf, 1941–

THE WORKS OF AELRED OF RIEVAULX

Adv	Sermo in adventu Domini
Fest Ben	Sermo in Festiuitate beati Benedicti Abbatis
Iesu	*De Iesu puero duodenni*
Inst incl	*De institutione inclusarum*

Lam D	*Lamentatio David Regis Scotie*
Nat Ben	Sermo in natali sancti Benedicti
Oner	*Homiliae de oneribus propheticis Isaiae*
Pur	Sermo in purificatione sanctae Mariae
Spec car	*Speculum caritatis*
Spir amic	*De spiritali amicitia*
Vita E	*Vita sancti Edwardi*

SCRIPTURAL ABBREVIATIONS

2 Chr	Second Chronicles
Col	Colossians
1 Cor	First Corinthians
2 Cor	Second Corinthians
Dn	Daniel
Dt	Deuteronomy
Eph	Ephesians
Ex	Exodus
Ezk	Ezekiel
Gal	Galatians
Heb	Hebrews
Is	Isaiah
Jb	Job
Jn	John
Jr	Jeremiah
1 [3] K	1 [3] Kings

Lk	Luke
Lv	Leviticus
Mt	Matthew
Prv	Proverbs
Ps(s)	Psalm(s)
Rom	Romans
Si	Sirach (Ecclesiasticus)
1 Thes	1 Thessalonians
Ws	Wisdom

AELRED AND HIS PRAYER [1]
AN INTRODUCTION TO AELRED'S
PASTORAL PRAYER

THROUGHOUT HIS WORKS Aelred shows himself to
be a gifted and careful writer, responsive to the works of
other writers and attentive to the needs of his audience.
He clearly takes pleasure in conveying his insights and concerns
gracefully as well as precisely. He varies his style and genre according to his subject and audience, sometimes telling a good
story or incorporating a speech or sermon within a narrative,
teaching sometimes through dialogue, sometimes through instruc-
tional imperatives or confessional prose. Like the earlier writers
he most admired and imitated, he understood the value of rhetoric
to a teacher, and as he wrote frequently, for many different occa-
sions and needs, he developed notable rhetorical power.

In none of his works, however, is he more lyrical, passionate,
and eloquent than in *Pastoral Prayer*. Speaking to God rather than
at least overtly to a human audience, he implies the human reality

1. This volume appears by permission of the Council of the Old Library of
Jesus College, Cambridge, and of *Cistercian Studies Quarterly* and its editor, Fr
Elias Dietz, OCSO. I am grateful for the assistance I have received from Fr Dietz,
Dr F. H. Willmoth (Assistant to the Keeper of the Old Library of Jesus College),
Fr Michael Casey, OCSO, Fr Charles Cummings, OCSO, Mark DelCogliano, Dr E.
Rozanne Elder, Brother Patrick Hart, OCSO, Dr Martin Jenni, Dom Bernard
Johnson, OCSO, and Fr Chrysogonus Waddell, OCSO. I am particularly indebted
to Dr Domenico Pezzini for the many insights I received from the Introduction
to his 2001 italian translation of *Oratio*. Full references to all citations appear in
the Select Bibliography, 59–65 below.

1

of those whom he has been called to guide and teach, voicing their own unvoiced prayer. His confession of inadequacy for the task he has been given is the confession that every honest man and woman must make. *Prayer* reveals not only the inner reality of the life of an abbot but the certain truth of each Christian and of each non-christian: 'I do not do the good I want, but the evil I do not want is what I do' (Rom 7:19). This work about christian duty, christian fear, christian candor, and christian love is the truth for all who read it, and Aelred's words enable all to speak that truth.

In *Prayer* Aelred beseeches God to give him 'a true and upright way of speaking and an eloquence of mouth' (§7) in order to build up his people. While the fulfillment of that prayer can only be inferred from what survives of his life and works, *Prayer* preserves a soaring echo of it, resonating through the centuries on parchment and paper, through pen and ink. The prayer is its own evidence of the union of the seeker with the sought: of the pastor with the flock whom he loves, of the writer with the readers of his prayer, of Aelred with the Good Shepherd to whom he prays. This prayer serves those who read and hear it today as it did the monks of Rievaulx: as evidence of the faith and humility of its writer, a token of his love for the sheep he kept, and a model and guide for those he never imagined. Finally *Prayer* today, as surely as when Aelred wrote it, reveals his hopes and heart, seeks to build the community he loved and served, and guides all of God's people, building each Christian's life 'in faith, hope and love, in chastity and humility, in patience and obedience, in fervor of spirit and devotion of mind' (§7).

The role of the abbot

To be worthy of the task of governing a monastery, the abbot must always remember what his title signifies and act as a superior should. He is believed to hold the place of Christ in the monastery, since he is addressed by a title of Christ, as the Apostle indicates: *You have received the spirit of adoption of sons by which we exclaim, abba, father . . . .* Let the abbot always remember that at the fearful judgment of God, not only his teaching but also his disciples' obedience will come under scrutiny. The abbot must, therefore, be aware that the shepherd will bear the blame wherever the father of the household finds that the sheep have yielded no profit. . . . The abbot must always remember what he is and remember what he is called, aware that more will be expected of a man to whom more has been entrusted. He must know what a difficult and demanding burden he has undertaken: directing souls and serving a variety of temperaments, coaxing, reproving and encouraging them as appropriate. He must so accommodate and adapt himself to each one's character and intelligence that he will not only keep the flock entrusted to his care from dwindling, but will rejoice in the increase of a good flock.[2]

With these words, Saint Benedict defines the heavy responsibility borne by each abbot as the shepherd of Christ's sheep and the one responsible to Christ, 'the father of the household', for the well-being of the community entrusted to him.[3] Later in the *Rule* Benedict explains that a good abbot must not merely fear divine judgment but also act out of love and compassion:

He is to imitate the loving example of the Good Shepherd who left the ninety-nine sheep in the mountains and went in search of the one sheep that had strayed. So great was his compassion for its weakness that he mercifully placed it on his sacred shoulders and so carried it back to the flock.[4]

2. RB 2.1–3, 6–7, 30–32; Fry 170–173, 176–177.

3. Claude Peifer notes that in the RB 'The abbot is identified as another Christ—as the one who represents him in the monastery—by application to him of the very titles that define the role of Christ himself'. Further, he says, Christ is always the *paterfamilias* ('father of the household') and the abbot 'only the shepherd to whom the *paterfamilias* entrusts his sheep' (351–352, 354).

4. Jn 10:11–15; Lk 15:4–5; RB 27.8–9; Fry 224–225. Peifer's discussion of 'Benedict's understanding of the abbot' (346–356) is a helpful background for *Prayer*.

Benedict's biblically resonant instructions underlie the *Pastoral Prayer* of Aelred of Rievaulx. As Aelred writes of his responsibility to teach, guide, and guard the monks of whom he is abbot, he also declares his love for them. But his words also speak to every Christian's desire to do God's will, fear of failure, struggle to love both God and neighbor, and discovery that truly loving either means truly loving both.

The abbot's concern for his monks is the central theme of *Prayer*. Intimately related to that theme is his anxiety about his ability to be a good shepherd and his need for Jesus' assistance. In confessing his own shortcomings the abbot exemplifies the combined effort and humility required of all of God's people, and by praying for the well-being of the monks, he manifests the love that may bind all members of any community to one another and to God. This prayer, which at first reading appears private and personal, is also an extended commentary on the role of the abbot as Benedict defines it in the *Rule,* especially in chapters 2, 27, and 64.[5] It is therefore Aelred's fullest statement of what it is to be an abbot—or, for that matter, to be a teacher, a parent, a priest, a lover, a friend.

AELRED'S LIFE

Aelred (1110–1167) passed his infancy and childhood with two brothers and perhaps a sister in the ancient Northumbrian town of Hexham, where his father, like his own father before him, was the priest of the church of Saint Andrew. Nothing is known of Aelred's formal education, although the quality of his written Latin and his familiarity with classical, patristic, and medieval writers indicates that he was well taught and widely read. His family's

5. Sister R. Penelope Lawson says that in *Prayer* Aelred 'intends to coalesce the ideals of Christ the Good Shepherd and Saint Benedict's Father Abbot into a single synthesis with his own shortcomings brought forward as a foil' ('Pastoral Prayer', CF 2:118 n. 66). While I was exploring *Prayer* as Aelred's commentary on the RB, Daniel M. La Corte was independently reaching many of the same conclusions; see his 'Aelred on Abbatial Responsibilites'.

long-time connections with Durham cathedral may have led him to study for a time in the cathedral school before going at the age of fourteen or fifteen to live at the court of King David I of Scotland. There he grew to adulthood with David's stepsons and son, and for some time he served as the court steward while discerning his life's vocation. As the church's growing insistence on clerical celibacy had made it impossible for him to follow his father and father's fathers as a secular priest, he may have considered settling into life-long service at court.[6]

But in 1134, responding to God's call to monastic life, Aelred entered the Yorkshire cistercian monastery of Rievaulx, founded just two years earlier. This daughter house of Saint Bernard's Clairvaux warmly welcomed the young Englishman, who in part because of his service to King David was already known to both Thurstan, the archbishop of York, and Walter Espec, the monastery's founder and patron.[7] David was also a patron of Rievaulx, according to an 1134 letter to him from Bernard: 'Our brothers who are at Rievaulx first experienced the inner parts of your mercy, those to whom you opened the treasury of your good will, upon whom you poured out the oil of mercy and the ointment of compassion'.[8] David's acquaintance with Thurstan, Walter Espec, and Bernard and his interest in Rievaulx may well have prompted Aelred to visit there, and David's patronage surely contributed to the enthusiastic welcome the monks there reportedly gave Aelred.

However Aelred came to Rievaulx, he had much to offer the young community, including a quick intelligence, generous spirit, compassionate heart, and profound faith. He was fluent—indeed eloquent—in Latin and French as well as English. His service at court had given him not only diplomatic experience but also

6. The best overview of Aelred's life remains Squire, *Aelred of Rievaulx*.

7. For a discussion of Aelred's entry into monastic life see Dutton, 'Conversion and Vocation'. See also Burton, 'Aux origines'. The familiar narrative of Aelred's entry into Rievaulx comes from Walter Daniel's *Life of Aelred*; see Vita A 5–7; CF 57:96–100.

8. Bernard, Ep 69; SBOp 8:478–479, here 478; James, *Letters*, 242 (Benedictine and SBOp edition 172).

5

practice in combining irenic humility and obedience with self-confidence and authority. He was the ideal person to contribute to the growth and stability of Rievaulx Abbey and of the Cistercian Order in England. His monastic brothers, obviously recognizing his gifts, in 1142 sent him as the representative of the abbot of Rievaulx with three northern prelates to Rome to appeal the election of William, King Stephen's nephew, as archbishop of York.[9]

After returning from Rome, Aelred was named novice master at Rievaulx. Within the year, however, he became the first abbot of Rievaulx's third daughter house, the Lincolnshire abbey of Saint Laurence of Revesby. Five years later, in 1147, the monks of Rievaulx elected him to be their third abbot. There he stayed until his death in January of 1167, building his community into what Walter Daniel described as 'the home of piety and peace, the abode of perfect love of God and neighbor'.[10]

Aelred wrote his first monastic treatise, *The Mirror of Charity,* in 1141 or 1142, perhaps in response to encouragement from Bernard of Clairvaux.[11] Over the next twenty-five years he wrote at least six other works of spiritual and monastic direction, seven historical and hagiographical treatises, many sermons, and, according to Walter Daniel, hundreds of letters, most of which are now lost.[12] Reginald of Durham reported that Aelred wrote verses on Saint Cuthbert,[13] and there is some reason to believe him to be the author of the hymn *Jesu Dulcis Memoria,* which appears in two early manuscripts of his works now in Oxford's Bodleian Library, one containing four of his historical works (Oxford MS Laud Misc.

9. Knowles, 'The Case of St William of York', 82–83.
10. Vita A 29; CF 57:118.
11. On the origins and date of *Mirror,* see Charles Dumont, Introduction, *Mirror of Charity,* 55–58; Emero Stiegman, 'Woods and Stones', 338–345.
12. Vita A 32; CF 57:120–122. The published editions and english translations of Aelred's works are listed in the second part of the Bibliography (60–61).
13. Reginald of Durham, *De admirandis Beati Cuthberti uirtutibus,* 22–28; see Squire, *Aelred of Rievaulx,* 5.

668) and one with his sermons *On the Prophetic Burdens of Isaiah* (Oxford MS Laud Misc. 648).[14]

Of Aelred's spiritual works, *Spiritual Friendship* was the most famous in the Middle Ages. This ciceronian dialogue between an abbot and first one and then two other monks explains human friendship as part of God's creation, containing within it God's unity and leading to God in this life and in beatitude. Another influential spiritual work was *The Formation of Anchoresses,* whose lengthy meditation on the humanity of Christ lies behind the popular medieval genre of lives of Christ and inspired both Bonaventure's *Tree of Life* and the *Spiritual Exercises* of Ignatius of Loyola.[15]

Aelred also had a particular interest in the history and political concerns of England. As a monastic historian he seems to have modeled himself on the Venerable Bede, whom he quotes in three of his seven historical works. From the Middle Ages until the late nineteenth century, Aelred was known primarily as a historian; his works place him among the twelfth-century historians whom M.-D. Chenu credits with developing a new kind of historical perspective recognizing the theological significance of human history.[16] Three of Aelred's works were prompted by contemporary events, such as a battle in the English Civil War (1135–1154) between King Stephen and the Empress Matilda, and the succession of Matilda's son Henry of Anjou to the throne in 1154 as Henry II.

Surviving manuscripts indicate that until well into the sixteenth century Aelred's two most popular works were *Genealogy of the Kings of the English,* directed to Henry of Anjou after Stephen designated him his heir, and *The Life of Saint Edward, King and Confessor,* written after Edward's 1161 canonization for the 1163 translation of his relics to a new shrine in Westminster Abbey. In these two works Aelred proclaimed Henry II the inheritor of the virtue and faith of the anglo-saxon kings of England and the

---

14. See Dumont, 'L'hymne "Dulcis Jesus Memoria" '; Wilmart, *Le 'Jubilus'.*
15. Dutton, 'Cistercian Source'.
16. Chenu, 'Theology and the New Awareness of History'; Dutton, 'A Historian's Historian'.

fulfillment of Edward's deathbed vision promising England peace after devastation.

THE DATE AND MANUSCRIPT OF PASTORAL PRAYER

No one knows when Aelred wrote *Prayer*.[17] For the most part his words sound like those of someone undertaking a new set of responsibilities, both desiring to carry out the role Jesus has given him and anxious about his ability to do so. Reading it as purely autobiographical and confessional thus suggests an early date of composition. But references to 'the weakness of my flesh' (§7) and assertions of profound love for the monks (§8) may indicate that Aelred was writing in old age, having grown into a love for his community deeper than what he could have known or even hoped for at the beginning of his abbacy. Perhaps for that reason, *Prayer* is usually regarded as a work of Aelred's age, written when physical frailty made it impossible to travel frequently or far but compensated him with time for reading, meditation, prayer, and writing, and when he had had ample time to reflect on Benedict's chapters about the responsibilities of abbots. The fact that Aelred apparently wrote most of his treatises during the final twelve years of his life, while often confined by illness, may also support a late date of composition.

In the centuries after Aelred's death the monks of Rievaulx held *Prayer* in great esteem. The work survives in a single parchment manuscript from the late twelfth or early thirteenth century, now Cambridge MS Jesus College Q.B. 17 (my MS. R).[18] Its binding today is modern leather over old boards, with the remnant of a clasp or strap and pin still attached. Small leather tabs on the outer edge of pages mark the beginnings of works. A small volume, it measures six by eight and a half inches and contains one hundred

17. I have discussed the date of *Prayer* in more detail in the Introduction to Mark DelCogliano, trans., '*The Pastoral Prayer*', 457–459.

18. For a reproduction of f. 108ᵛ and a discussion of the manuscript, see Waddell, 'Notes', ii, 12. See also James, *Catalogue*, 43–56.

thirty-seven folios written in several twelfth- and thirteenth-century hands, some in a single column, others in two columns, with from thirty to thirty-eight lines per page.

The manuscript begins with two versions of the monastery's library catalogue, the original and one that David N. Bell describes as 'little more than an abbreviated version'.[19] It also contains about fourteen other works in a variety of genres. The physical variation among the items shows the manuscript to have been compiled from various sources over several decades rather than being copied from a single exemplar. M. R. James labels it a *'Tractatus Miscellanei'*, and Chrysogonus Waddell describes it as a commonplace book.[20]

Red, green, and blue inks have been used in various ways throughout the manuscript. In the library catalogues large rubricated letters from A to Q indicate the library's grouping of manuscripts; rubrication also marks the first letter of many titles and names of authors. Elsewhere in the manuscript red and green initials appear at the beginning of new texts or sections, with rubrication used for *incipits* and *explicits.* Some initials contain blue scrolling, and the official cistercian documents on ff. 100–108 have initials in red, green, and blue.

Jesus College MS Q.B. 17 is an important record of cistercian history. The two catalogues (ff. 1–6) precede a number of short theological excerpts, some sermons (ff. 7–96ᵛ), and, on ff. 97–99, *Oratio pastoralis (Prayer)*. Next come several historically important cistercian documents, including the *Exordium parvum* (ff. 100–105), the first nine chapters of the *Carta caritatis prior* (ff. 105–107), Pope Innocent II's 1132 privilege to the Cistercians (ff. 107–108), a brief letter from Stephen Harding to the abbot of Sherburne (f. 108ᵛ), and Saint Bernard's letter *Inter cetera que optime,* on the

19. The two library catalogues have been edited several times, most recently by Bell, *Libraries,* 87–137 and plates 3 and 4. In the essay introducing his edition Bell discusses the relationship between the two versions of the catalogue and explains the sixteen categories of volumes in the library. Aelred's works were in category D, with the works of Bernard and Anselm.

20. James, *Catalogue,* 43; Waddell, 'Notes', 12.

promulgation of the revised cistercian antiphonary from 1147 or shortly before,[21] followed by an anonymous treatise presenting the rationale for the revision and a description in dialogue form of the cistercian psalm-tones (ff. 109–116^v).

Oratio pastoralis is a short treatise in a gothic hand occupying five pages (two and a half leaves), written in a single thirty-five-line column. After the rubricated *incipit,* which stands alone on the first line of folio 97^r, the text begins with a single large red initial O, three and a half lines high and with minimal interior decorative scrolling. No other decoration appears in the text, and no initials or paragraph marks indicate any textual divisions. Two hands are responsible for the work, the scribe's and that of a later corrector.

The manuscript identifies the monastery to which it belongs four times within its pages; besides the library catalogue's title on f. 1^r, '*Hi sunt libri sancte Marie Rieuallensis*', the phrase '*Liber sancte Marie Rieuallensis*' appears on ff. 7^v, 47^v, and 109^r. The manuscript thus signals the significance of *Prayer* for the Rievaulx monks, who preserved it as a memorial of their abbot, 'a family legacy', in the words of André Wilmart.[22] The table of contents inside the front cover of the manuscript identifies Aelred as both the author of *Prayer* and the abbot of Rievaulx. That table of contents was probably written by a fourteenth-century chancellor of Lincoln, V. Dupin, whose name and title, dated 1330, appear on f. 43va, probably in his own hand.

Additions in two hands preceding and following *Prayer* also identify Aelred as the author. At the top of f. 97^r, above the first line of the work, a thirteenth-century hand writes 'The prayer of venerable Aelred, Abbot of Rievaulx, meant for prelates and especially abbots'.[23] Just below, a hand of the fourteenth or fifteenth

---

21. Waddell, 'Origin', 192–193 n. 5.

22. Wilmart, ed., 'L'Oraison', 271.

23. *Oracio venerabilis Aelredi Abbatis Rieuallensis propria prelatorum maxime abbatum.*

century adds 'composed and used by him'.[24] Two brief quotations from Aelred, probably in that same fourteenth- or fifteenth-century hand, follow the text on f. 99 and echo *Prayer*'s words about his love for his monks.[25] A centered heading to the first passage identifies it as coming from one of his now-lost letters:

> In his twenty-first epistle he says thus:
> Listen: before highest heaven I swear and testify that I bear on my conscience no burden of ever having intended to take vengeance on anyone—I mean not merely by speaking or shouting, but even by glaring angrily or looking askance at someone.[26]

The second is an excerpt from Walter Daniel's description of Aelred's death, with a heading identifying its context:

> At the end, with his brothers standing by, he said thus:
> I have lived with a good conscience among you, for as I lie here, as you see, at the point of death, my soul calls God to witness that never since I received this habit of religion has the malice, detraction, or quarrel of any man ever kindled in me any feeling against him strong enough to last the day in the domicile of my heart.[27]

Wilmart notes the significance of these passages for Aelred's reputation at Rievaulx: 'these fragments [*morceaux*] prove that the

24. *ab eo composita et vsitata*
25. Both excerpts appear in the introduction to the first edition of the work; the words *irato vvltu* are missing from the first excerpt (Wilmart, 'L'Oraison', 271–272). Wilmart corrected this omission in 'Le texte', 74.
26. *In Epistola sua. xxius sic ait. Ecce in celo testis meus et conscius meus in excelso quia non est in consciencia mea quod ex quo onus hoc nomenque suscepi tali intencione vt me vlciscerer contra aliquem non dico aliquid egerim vel dixerim. sed nec oculos quidem in transuersum irato vvltu iactauerim.* (My transcriptions follow manuscript capitalization and orthography but silently expand abbreviations.)
27. *In extremis fratribus astantibus; sic ait. Ego cum bona consciencia conuersatus sum inter vos. quia deum testem inuoco in animam meam vtpote constitutus vt cernitis in articulo mortis. quod nuncquam postquam habitum Religionis accepi cuiuslibet hominis malicia vel detraccione aut litigio in illum exarsi aliqua commocione. que diei finem in domicilio cordis mei expectare preualuisset* (Vita A 57–58; CF 57:134–135).

memory of him, of his virtues, and, notably, of his gentleness, was not lost at the end of the Middle Ages.'[28]

André Wilmart (1876–1941) discovered *Prayer* and published it in a diplomatic edition in *Revue Bénédictine* in 1925.[29] He divided the text into ten numbered sections and appended meticulous notes identifying erasures, marginal additions, and possible textual errors, consistently signaling and explaining his emendations while sometimes suggesting alternative readings to those of the manuscript. He also provided citations for Aelred's biblical, patristic, and liturgical quotations and allusions. In 1929 he printed a list of errors in that first version and later printed the corrected edition in a collection of his articles, *Auteurs spirituels et textes dévots du moyen âge latin*.[30]

Over the decades Wilmart's edition has been repeatedly reprinted with minor alterations and translated into German, Dutch, English, French, Spanish, and Italian.[31] In 1961 Charles Dumont printed his French translation with Wilmart's edition on facing pages. He identified Wilmart as the editor (as most others had not), incorporated most but not all of Wilmart's corrections, and retained some of Wilmart's notes and commentary on editorial decisions while replacing manuscript punctuation with syntactic punctuation. Dumont also retained Wilmart's ten textual divisions while adding additional unnumbered paragraphs.[32]

In 1971 Anselm Hoste and C. H. Talbot reprinted Dumont's version of Wilmart's edition among Aelred's ascetic works in Corpus Christianorum, Continuatio Mediævalis 1. They identified Wilmart as its editor but in the apparatus noted several manuscript readings neither recorded by Wilmart in 1925 or 1929 nor in-

---

28. Wilmart, 'L'Oraison', 271.

29. Wilmart, 'L'Oraison', 271–272. For a complete overview of the editorial tradition, see Dutton, 'Oratio', 299–302.

30. Wilmart, ed., *Auteurs spirituels*, 287–298.

31. The best-known english translation is Lawson's, first printed in 1955 and reprinted in CF 2 in 1971.

32. Dumont, trans., *La prière pastorale*, 171–203.

cluded in any subsequent version of the edition.[33] For example, both Wilmart and Dumont omitted *sit* from the manuscript's *sublimitas sit* (§3), but Hoste and Talbot included it and by noting its presence in the manuscript tacitly indicated its previous omission. Unfortunately, new errors slipped into the CCCM text. Hoste and Talbot printed the manuscript reading *inpendar* as *impendat* (§7) and the manuscript's *adiuuet* as *adiuet* (§8). A few of Wilmart's transcription errors also persist in the CCCM text, e.g., the reading *sancta* in place of the correct *facta* in §2.

THE MONASTIC COMMUNITY

The chief concern of *Prayer* is the abbot's responsibility for the members of the monastic community, explored in Aelred's own voice. From beginning to end Aelred asks that Jesus assist him as he labors to guide, protect, and serve the monks. He proclaims his love for them and identifies them as Jesus' own people, whom Jesus has created and led into monastic life. They exist, he says, entirely because of Jesus' loving acts:

> I beg you to tell me this, sweet Lord: is this not your family, your own people, whom you led out of Egypt for a second time, whom you created, whom you redeemed? At long last you have gathered them from various lands and given those of like mind a home to live in. (§3)

With this language Aelred defines the community as a new Israel. While baptism rescues all Christians from the Egypt of bondage to sin and death and introduces them to the promised land of salvation, the monk through profession undergoes a second exodus, from the Egypt of the world into monastic life.[34] By twice saving the members of the community, Jesus has made them doubly his

33. Hoste and Talbot, eds., 'Oratio Pastoralis', 757–763. The half-title page contains the phrase 'Ad fidem editionis A. Wilmart'.
34. See Aelred, SS 6, 8 (Fest Ben), CCCM 2A:53–60, 65–69; CF 58:129–141, 147–154. See also Bernard, S div 11.3; SBOp 6/1:126.

own people, the sheep of his pasture. At the same time, he has given them a shepherd, the abbot who guides and protects them on behalf of the father of the family, the Good Shepherd.[35]

Aelred also emphasizes here that the members of the community have come together not by happenstance but as fulfillment of Jesus' purpose for them. Those who had been no people, scattered among the peoples of the world, have now been gathered and made into a people united in purpose, understanding, and practice, dwelling together in common life.

In this work the defining aspect of the community is that it belongs to Jesus, not only created and gathered by him but also belonging to him: his flock, his family, his very own people. The beginning of *Prayer,* in accord with the controlling image of both Jesus and the abbot as shepherds, refers to the members of the community three times as sheep belonging to Jesus: 'your sheep', 'the sheep of your pasture'. This image echoes not only Benedict's direction to abbots but also the various biblical passages referring to the people of Israel as God's sheep. It characterizes them in terms of their group identity and their dependence on their shepherd for food, shelter, and protection.

Quickly, however, Aelred changes the reference, now four times identifying the community as Jesus' family, united not merely by common need or a shared home and shepherd but by their relationship with one another, with Jesus implicitly their brother and father—their *paterfamilias.* As a family they are more closely connected to one another and to Jesus, but they are also differentiated, with a greater variety of roles and more responsibility to and for one another.[36]

---

35. Cf. Peifer, 351–353.

36. Aelred's emphasis on the monks of Rievaulx as a family anticipates Pope Leo II's 1902 reference to the 'Cistercian Family' and Pope John Paul II's 1998 letter 'To the Members of the Cistercian Family'. Dom Olivier Quenardel, ocso, abbot of Cîteaux, has examined Benedict's encouragement in RB 35 of mutual support and help among members of the monastic community; he focuses especially on the terms *servire, invicem, solatium,* and *mandatum* ('Cistercian Diakonia').

Aelred then defines the community in a different way, as Jesus' people—*tuus populus, tuus populus peculiaris.* He uses this phrase seven times, first as an extension, or perhaps a reconsideration, of the image of family: *familia tua, populus tuus peculiaris.* In this way he again defines them as a new Israel, gathered together apart from the people of the nations, with Jesus alone their God.

So Aelred develops and defines the community as composed of those whom Jesus created and called together to be his own. While he never alters his insistence that the community belongs to Jesus, he gradually reshapes his image of their identity. At first they are an undifferentiated flock, identical in their hooded cowls of undyed wool and requiring from their abbot the essentials of life. They then become a family, related to one another. And finally they are a people, a new nation, ruled by a sovereign and with responsibilities even beyond those determined by their family standing. Aelred does not work out the implications of these three terms or the stages of his understanding, but when he begins to call the community Jesus' family he ceases to refer to them as sheep, and once he names them Jesus' people he no longer calls them a family.

The pervasive themes of *Prayer*—the relationship of the shepherd and the flock, the abbot's desire for Jesus' assistance so that he may rule his community wisely and well, and the abbot's obedience to and imitation of Jesus—all reflect the mutual responsibility and love of the abbot and the monks, gathered, guarded, and ruled by Jesus. Aelred's prayer for himself as shepherd does not merely imply but necessitates a flock. As a shepherd who has no flock is no shepherd, an abbot is an abbot only because he has monks, and monks without an abbot are no monks at all.[37] In

---

His study helpfully complements Aelred's treatment of the community in *Prayer.*

37. Cf. RB 1.2, 6–8; Fry 168–171. According to Peifer, Benedict regards the *sarabaites* 'as false cenobites because they lack the one element most necessary to a real *coenobium*: a shepherd (1.8). Hence the monasteries in which they live are not "the Lord's" sheepfolds but only their own; he is not the *paterfamilias* of these sheep, for their representative, the abbot, is not there to act for him on their behalf' (352).

Prayer Aelred asks nothing for himself, for his own physical well-being or spiritual growth or salvation—only the ability to do what is expected of him and to care adequately for those who have been given to him.

In order to fulfill his responsibility to the community, however, the abbot must differentiate among its members, identifying their differences of character and personality. Aelred therefore asks Jesus to assist him to understand and reach out to each member of the community, to be the shepherd who calls each sheep by name (Jn 10:3). In this request he moves from generalized emotion, powerful but potentially vagrant, toward satisfaction of Benedict's requirement that the abbot respond to 'a variety of temperaments' in his community and 'accommodate and adapt himself to each one's character and intelligence'.[38]

Benedict's words echo Saint Paul's exhortation to the Christians of Rome to 'rejoice with those who rejoice and weep with those who weep' and to the Thessalonians to 'restrain the restless, comfort the discouraged, and support the weak', as well as his claim to have become 'all things to all people so that I might by all means save some.'[39] It is no wonder that such great monastic writers as Cassian, the author of the *Rule of the Master,* and Gregory the Great incorporated this same idea into their works,[40] and that Bernard of Clairvaux reminded Rainald, the new abbot of Foigny, of his responsibility for those with particular needs: 'You are especially the abbot of those whom you find sad, faint-hearted, and discontented. By consoling, encouraging, and admonishing you do your duty, you bear your burden. And by bearing that burden you carry those who need healing to health.'[41]

---

38. RB 2.31, 2.30; Fry, 176–177.
39. Rom 12:15; 1 Thes 5:14; 1 Cor 9:22.
40. See, e.g., Cassian, *Collations* 17.20; Cassian, *Collationes XXIIII,* 481–486; *La Règle du Maître* 2.11–12; CS 6:112; Gregory, *Liber* 3.prol.; *The Book of Pastoral Rule,* 24–71, here 24.
41. Ep 73.2; SBOp 7:180; James, *Letters,* 107 (76).

Aelred too expresses the abbot's obligation to care for the monks in all their needs, using words like those of Paul, Benedict, and Bernard. Thereby he makes it clear that the abbot needs God's help in his efforts:

> Let me learn, let your Spirit teach me, to console the sorrowing, to strengthen the fainthearted, to set the fallen upright, to be weak with the weak, to be indignant with the scandalized, to become all things to all people in order to win them all. . . . teach me, sweet Lord, to admonish the disturbed, to console the fainthearted, to support the weak, and to accommodate myself to each one's character, disposition, inclinations, aptitude, or simplicity, according to the place and time, as seems best to you. (§7)

The Abbot as Shepherd, King, and Imitator of Jesus

Although *Prayer* essentially explores Benedict's requirements that the abbot love and guard the members of his community, it is usually read as a personal portrait of its author. One reason for that interpretation is the confessional tone of the work, beginning as it does with the words 'to you a shepherd now cries, a poor and pitiable shepherd . . . this no-good shepherd. To you he cries, worried about himself, worried about your sheep' (§1). A contributing factor, however, is Wilmart's titles for his ten divisions of *Prayer,* titles that ignore both the pervasive influence of the *Rule* and the centrality of the abbot's concern for the community:

> One could define these parts in this way . . . : appeal to the Good Shepherd, act of contrition, examination of the abbot's charge, introduction to the double prayer, prayer for his needs, request for wisdom, request for assistance for the well-being of all, prayer for subordinates and request for the Holy Spirit, prayer for temporal well-being, and commendation of himself to God.[42]

42. Wilmart, 'L'Oraison', 266.

All subsequent printings of the text in Latin or vernacular translations (including those here) have retained Wilmart's divisions, often
with his titles.

By focusing the reader's attention on the abbot who prays
rather than on the community that is the subject of his prayer,
Wilmart's titles have helped to define *Prayer* as fundamentally
private, an appeal that the reader merely overhears. That reading,
however, overlooks Aelred's concern with the way the *Rule* defines
the abbot's charge and his insistence on the abbot's responsibility
to serve and love his community. Aelred is explicit that he prays
on behalf of those whom Jesus has appointed him to guide: 'O
God of mercy, hear me—for their sake! I pray to you for their
sake, compelled by the duty of my office, urged on by my attachment to them, yet quickened with joy when I contemplate your
kindness' (§8).

In *Prayer* as in the *Rule of Benedict,* two biblical images define
the abbot's responsibility: that of the nurturing and guiding shepherd to Jesus' flock, and that of the king who rules Jesus' people
with wisdom. In both roles the abbot is above all to imitate Jesus—
'to remember what his title signifies'—not only protecting and
guiding the community but also giving himself for them in love.

These two images are fundamentally the same. In biblical
terms, the one who shepherds God's people is also their king, and
as both shepherd and king he is an image of Jesus. This conflation
of roles reflects the fact that because of God's transformation of
the shepherd boy David into the great king of Israel, biblical authors wrote of the kings of Judah as shepherds of the people.
Speaking in God's name, the Hebrew prophets condemned these
kings as bad shepherds, who fed themselves while exposing their
flocks as prey to wild animals, to the nations that devoured the
people.[43]

This language also governs God's promise through the prophets that God himself will reunite his people:

43. See Peifer, 351–352.

18

Woe to the shepherds who destroy and scatter the sheep of my pasture! says the Lord. Therefore thus says the Lord, the God of Israel, concerning the shepherds who shepherd my people: It is you who have scattered my flock, and have driven them away, and you have not attended to them. . . . Then I myself will gather the remnant of my flock out of all the lands where I have driven them, and I will bring them back to their fold, and they shall be fruitful and multiply. I will raise up shepherds over them who will shepherd them, and they shall not fear any longer, or be dismayed, nor shall any be missing, says the Lord.[44]

When the psalmist proclaims 'The Lord is my shepherd' (*Dominus regit me* [Ps 23:1]) or 'Give ear, oh Shepherd of Israel' (*Qui regis Israël intende* [Ps 80:1]), he acknowledges that God himself is the ruler and shepherd of his people and, in Christian interpretation, looks forward to the time when Jesus, the Good Shepherd, will come to his people.[45]

The images develop in different ways in the *Rule* and in *Prayer*, however. In the *Rule* Benedict insists on the responsibility borne by those chosen by God as shepherds over his people and representatives of the Good Shepherd. Reminding them of the danger to them and their flock if they fail, he quotes the prophet Ezekiel to emphasize the significance of their role:

It is the abbot's responsibility to have great concern and to act with all speed, discernment and diligence in order not to lose any of the sheep entrusted to him. He should realize that he has undertaken care of the sick, not tyranny

44. Jer 23:1–4

45. The Latin verb *rego*, used, e.g., in Pss 23 and 80, translates the Hebrew verb *ra'ah*; in both languages the verb means both 'to rule' and 'to shepherd'. In the Old Testament the verb conveys the dual responsibility of the king; in the RB and in *Prayer* that same ambiguity informs the abbot's role. Benedict uses the verb *regere* in RB 2.31 in reference to directing souls (*regere animas*), and Aelred uses it seven times in *Prayer*, twice in reference to Jesus' rule and five times to his own responsibility 'to guide your people' (*regere populum tuum*).

over the healthy. Let him also fear the threat of the Prophet in which God says: *What you saw to be fat you claimed for yourselves, and what was weak you cast aside* [Ezk 34:3–4].[46]

Although Benedict never writes of the abbot as a king, his use here of Ezekiel's words to the shepherd-kings demands that the abbot direct and exercise authority over the community even as he nurtures and protects—that he be a good ruler as well as a good shepherd.

Aelred is more explicit than Benedict in working out the implications of the biblical trope. For half of *Prayer* he writes of the abbot as shepherd of the sheep, declaring his responsibility for nurturing, teaching, caring for, praying for, and safeguarding the monks. Even when he stops referring to them as sheep, he treats the shepherd's responsibilities as paramount. But halfway through *Prayer,* at the beginning of §6, he turns his attention to the abbot as king, the guide of his people, the one who exercises authority and discipline. As Benedict directs the abbot not to preside over (*praeesse*) his monks but to profit them (*prodesse*),[47] Aelred's model for the abbot is Solomon, who as a new king asked for wisdom with which to guide God's people.[48] Aelred too asks for wisdom in order to guide his community:

And so, sweet Lord, I ask to be given not gold or silver or jewels, but rather wisdom so that I may know how to guide your people [*regere populum tuum*]. O font of wisdom, send her forth from the throne of your glory so that she may be with me, toil with me, work with me, speak in me, and bring my thoughts and my words, all my undertakings and decisions, into harmony with your good will, to the honor of your name, for their progress and my salvation. (§6)

46. Lk 15:5; RB 27.5–9; Fry 224–225.
47. Aelred uses this phrase twice in *Prayer,* taking it from RB 64.8: *sciatque sibi oportere prodesse magis quam praeesse*; Fry 282–283.
48. 2 Chr 1:7–12; cf. 1 [3] Kgs 3:5–9.

Aelred's definition here of the abbot's kingship rejects any claim to power over the people. The king is still, in fact, the shepherd, called to guide Jesus' people, as the phrase *regere populum tuum* indicates. The true beneficiaries of the abbot's wisdom are the people.

Always, however, Benedict and Aelred say, the abbot is to be to the community as Jesus is to his people. At the beginning of *Prayer* Aelred not only invokes Jesus as shepherd and identifies himself with Jesus but declares his pastoral responsibility to the community, Jesus' own flock: 'he is nevertheless the shepherd of your sheep, such as he is' (§1). Again, when he identifies himself with Solomon, he asks Jesus for the wisdom to guide his people. At the end of the work he portrays the abbot not only as the one required to guard and guide the sheep but also as the one called to serve Jesus and therefore to serve his people: 'make me, your servant, the dependable dispenser, the discerning distributor, the prudent provider of all that you have given. . . . I am your servant and, because of you, also theirs' (§9). So Aelred ends *Prayer* not by celebrating his own rise from serving a king to ruling a monastery but by declaring himself a servant to the High King above all kings, and so to His people.

The abbot also imitates Christ in offering himself to his community. Throughout *Prayer* Aelred repeatedly asks to imitate Christ's offering of himself:

> Still more, may I find happiness in being utterly spent for them. Let it be done in this way, my Lord, let it be done in this way! All my feeling, all my speaking, all my rest and all my work, all my action and all my thought, all my success and all my hardship, all my death and all my life, all my health and sickness—all that I am, all that gives me life, all that I feel, all that I discern—let all this be expended upon them in all its entirety and entirely spent for their benefit, for the benefit of those for whom you yourself did not consider it unworthy to be utterly spent. (§7)

The abbot's prayer for the community thus entails a self-conscious *imitatio Christi*. As a shepherd the abbot's model is Jesus. As a king, his antecedent is Solomon, an Old Testament type of

Jesus; again, Jesus is his model. So Aelred proclaims a desire to follow his lord in every way, always manifesting Jesus' care for and offering of himself for Jesus' people. He not only reflects Benedict's requirements for an abbot but also provides a theologically and scripturally grounded understanding of abbacy, with the abbot always aware that he represents Jesus in the monastery and that he must also seek to be like him.

Jesus in *Prayer*

While the central theme of *Prayer* is the relationship between the abbot and his community, the work also contains a powerful characterization of Jesus as the eternal shepherd and king of his people, the One who has redeemed them through his death on the cross. In the course of *Prayer* Aelred repeatedly addresses Jesus not as the man of Nazareth but as God himself, the Lord of creation, addressing him in names revealing his lordship as well as his mercy and tenderness to his people. After the initial address to the Good Shepherd, Aelred calls him *Iesus meus* once, then nine times *Domine,* another nine times *dulcis Domine,* four times *mi Domine* or *Domine mi,* four times *Domine Deus meus* or *Deus meus,* once *misericors Deus noster,* and once each *piissime, spes mea, inspector cordis mea, fons misericordie, fons pietatis,* and *fons sapientie.* The final address encompasses them all: *dulcissimo Domino nostro.* The effect of this repetition and variation of names for God Incarnate recalls the music of the psalms, culminating in a cry of joy proclaiming Jesus as one with the Father and the Holy Spirit, the great God of mercy and wisdom, the God of all his people.

Aelred several times does address Jesus in his humanity, however, as the lover and saviour of humankind. The first words of *Prayer* call him not only good but also merciful and loving— *clemens, pie*—familiar words addressed to Jesus' mother Mary in the great antiphon-hymn *Salve Regina.*[49] Later Aelred addresses

49. As Bede Lackner notes, although the *Salve* had become part of the Cluniac liturgy in 1031, until the thirteenth century Cistercians sang it only four

Jesus as 'font of mercy' (§3) and 'font of loving tenderness' (§5) and explains that he dares to pray 'on the basis of your great mercy' (§4). He also specifically appeals to Jesus through his humanity: 'in the power of your name . . . and by the power of the mystery of your sacred humanity' (§5).

Aelred echoes the traditional association of the second person of the Trinity with Wisdom when he addresses him as the font of wisdom (§6) and defines him as the giver of wisdom.[50] In this context Aelred links Jesus the crucified saviour with Jesus as Wisdom: 'Here, sweet Lord, here in your sight are your own people. Before their eyes are your cross and the signs of your passion. . . . . And so, sweet Lord, I ask to be given . . . wisdom so that I may know how to guide your people' (§6).

Aelred also addresses Jesus as physician, teacher, and father, terms that Benedict applies to the abbot.[51] Aelred, however, assigns these terms not to himself but to Jesus: 'I place all my hope in your loving tenderness, O most merciful, because I know that you will look upon me either as a loving physician who will heal me or as a most kind teacher who will set me straight or as a most indulgent father who will pardon me' (§5). This inversion of the expected relationship between abbot and monk, with the abbot now needing care from the *paterfamilias,* shows Jesus as the abbot's model in these roles as well as in those of shepherd and king. Aelred further identifies Jesus as the abbatial archetype whose own voice is heard behind Benedict's in the *Rule*. Quoting from the chapter on the election of the abbot, Aelred refers to the

---

times a year, on the feasts of the Annunciation, Purification, Assumption, and Christmas (Lackner, 'Liturgy', 32). Aelred is clearly familiar with it, however, addressing Mary as '*o pia, o dulcis Maria*' in a chapter discourse for the Feast of the Annunciation (S 58.24; CCCM 2B:113).

50. Elsewhere Aelred similarly refers to the distribution of power, wisdom, and goodness among the Father, the Son, and the Holy Spirit (e.g., SS 67.4, 13, and 68.6 [Pent]; CCCM 2B:182, 184, 192).

51. E.g., RB 27.2, 28.2 (physician); 2.24, 3.6 (teacher); 7.44, 46.5, 49.8–10 (father); see Peifer 352, 357–367. On the abbot as teacher and father, see also La Corte, 'Abbot'.

community as 'those you bid me to profit rather than to preside over' (§6), tacitly defining Benedict's requirements as Jesus' own.

Most powerfully, however, the Lord whom Aelred addresses in *Prayer* is the Triune God, not only Son but also Father and Holy Spirit. So he links Jesus not only with Wisdom but also with the God of the Old Testament when he identifies him both as the source of Solomon's wisdom and as the crucified lord:

> One of the men of old once begged to be given the wisdom to know how to guide your people. . . . you listened to his voice, even though it was before you died on the cross, even though it was before you displayed that wonderful act of love to your people. (§6)

The people whom Solomon sought to rule in wisdom, Aelred says, were already the people of Jesus, who would suffer crucifixion on their behalf, as are the people for whom Aelred now prays: 'Here, sweet Lord, here in your sight are your own people. . . . You have entrusted them to this sinner, your trifling servant, for guidance' (§6).

Jesus is also the one in *Prayer* who gives the Holy Spirit and the Spirit's gifts. Praying for spiritual fulfillment, Aelred requests not a more intimate relationship with Jesus the man, but the presence of his Spirit:

> Let your good and sweet Spirit descend into my heart and prepare in it a dwelling place for himself, cleansing it from all defilement of flesh and spirit and pouring into it an increase of faith, hope, and love and a disposition of compunction, loving tenderness, and kindness. (§5)

The result of this in-dwelling, Aelred says, will be an increase in his ability to love Jesus: 'let him bestow upon me the fervor and discernment to love and praise you, to pray to you and meditate on you, the dedication and capability to have all my thoughts and deeds be in harmony with you, and perseverance in all these things until the very end of my life' (§5).

But Aelred does not here express a desire to linger in union with or meditation upon the Holy Spirit; instead he turns back to the community's necessity. His requests are only briefly personal, prompted mostly by the responsibilities of his office: 'Now I certainly need all these things for myself because of who I am, O my hope. There are other things that I need not only because of who I am but also because of those you bid me to profit rather than to preside over' (§6). The abbot who remembers who he is and whom he serves, as Benedict requires, sacrifices even the desire for personal spiritual experience in order to serve Jesus and his people.[52]

The end of *Prayer* fulfills the abbot's prayer to expend himself for the community as Aelred leaves the sheep alone with their true shepherd and lord. The last sentences also reveal that in assisting the abbot Jesus enables the abbot to grow into his likeness. While the beginning of *Prayer* calls attention to the great distance between the Good Shepherd and his representative, the poor, no-good shepherd, here Aelred says that they share responsibility for the community.

The Pastoral Prayer ends as it began, with Jesus as the shepherd of the people, the sweetest of lords, who holds and protects his people. In the last lines Aelred becomes explicitly the temporary substitute for Jesus, the one who has served Jesus for just a little while by caring for his people: 'I, however, entrust them into your holy hands and to your loving providence, in the hope that not even one of them will be snatched out of your hand or out of the hand of your servant to whom you have entrusted them' (§10). *Prayer* ends with the monks once more in the hands of Jesus, who gives them safety, happiness on the path to holiness, and perseverance.

Finally Jesus alone reigns as shepherd and king, caretaker and guardian of his family, those who rest in his safekeeping. He is the one who lives for all eternity, on whose behalf the abbot has served and to whom the abbot now commends the community. He is the Triune God, Father, Son, and Holy Spirit, 'our sweetest Lord, you who live and reign forever and ever' (§10).

---

52. Aelred also requires the sacrifice of spiritual delight to the needs of the community in *Jesus as a Boy of Twelve,* when after reaching the contemplative joys of Jerusalem the seeker must return to care for his brethren (Iesu 3.30–31; CCCM 1:276–277; CF 2:37–39).

A powerfully personal voice runs throughout *Prayer,* ostensibly an uncurtained window to the heart and mind of the writer as he reveals his own weakness, sin, and fear of being a poor shepherd to God's sheep. The writer's declaration of unfitness for his abbatial responsibilities is for many readers the most memorable aspect of the work; its lyrical words convey an awareness not only of what God requires of the abbot but also of how little he feels himself able to do it:

> Though I have far too little concern for myself, you bid me to be concerned for others; though in every way I lack what it takes to pray for my sins, my own sins, you bid me pray for others; though I myself am far too un-taught, you bid me teach others. Wretched me! What have I done? What have I undertaken? What have I agreed to? (§3)

Prayer's emotional impact resides in this candor, as Aelred confesses his inadequacy for the task he has accepted and passionately declares his desire to love and serve Jesus' people. His thoughts and words rise with the simplicity and rhetorical power available to only the best, the most gifted and most diligent, of writers. Thus even as *Prayer* seems to reveal the unselfconsciously private self of the one who prays—his sense of his own faults, his desire to serve Jesus in the place where Jesus has put him, his love and concern for his monks—it also reveals Aelred's rhetorical skills and his determination to make this work worthy of all the members of its audience: of God, who hears his words, and of those who read them. As he prays for aid in adapting himself to the various needs of his monks, he asks also for the rhetorical ability to serve them: 'Grant me a true and upright way of speaking and an eloquence of mouth to build them up in faith, hope, and love, in chastity and humility, in patience and obedience, in fervor of spirit and devotion of mind' (§7).

Aelred wrote most of his spiritual works with a marked note of authority, often portraying himself as in some sense a teacher and guide. He appears in *The Mirror of Charity* as a novice master counseling a novice, in *Jesus as a Boy of Twelve* and *Spiritual Friendship* as an abbot answering questions of other monks, and in *The Genealogy of the Kings of the English* as an advisor to a future king. *Prayer,* however, reveals him as an ordinary, frightened, vulnerable man—the only such portrait in his works. Here his usual tone of self-confidence yields to the truth that all abbots, all priests, all teachers know of the self usually veiled by the office. He confesses his unfitness to be an abbot, his acceptance of God's will that he be one, and his deep love for the monks, whom he seeks to serve:

> O God of mercy, hear me—for their sake! I pray to you for their sake, compelled by the duty of my office, urged on by my attachment to them, yet quickened with joy when I contemplate your kindness. . . . You know how I want to profit them in love rather than to preside over them, to be placed in a humble position below them but also to be held in affection among them as one of them. (§8)

But the compelling personal voice that governs *Prayer* is not unique to Aelred. The work cannot be read as transparently autobiographical, though there is no reason to doubt his honesty in confessing himself unprepared to be vicar of Christ and guardian of Christ's family—what honest person would not tremble before such responsibility? Still, in its humility, in its rhetorical power, and often even in its phrasing, *Prayer* reveals the influence of great spiritual writers of Aelred's time and before. For in this work Aelred adapts a newly popular genre and relies on the works of his predecessors even while incorporating into his own work God's and Benedict's requirements for the shepherd of Jesus' sheep.

The genre of *Prayer* is one familiar to both Aelred and his readers. Over the centuries authors had confessed their weakness to God while intending their words for a human audience, expressing their honest yearning and fear while also declaring human dependence on God. Their voices resonate throughout *Prayer*. As Aelred proclaims his own eagerness to serve and his fear of failure, he remembers the words of Paul—'I do not do the good I want, but the evil I do not want is what I do'[53]—and of Augustine of Hippo: 'Allow me to speak before your mercy, though I am but dust and ashes.'[54]

In the eleventh century, such public confessions developed into a new genre of written prayers and meditations, still ultimately intended for public readership but written as intimate communications.[55] Most memorably, John of Fécamp (d. 1078) and Anselm of Canterbury (c. 1033–1109) addressed God or a saint in short poetic prayers and meditations written in a strikingly personal tone. Benedicta Ward explains such works as intentionally private, unlike public liturgical prayer: 'The *Prayers and Meditations* are not meant to be read in the congregation of the faithful but in the secret chamber, not only in the inner room of the heart, but literally apart, in solitude'.[56]

John and Anselm both anticipate Aelred's *Prayer* when they confess their unsuitability for the roles God has given them. In 'Prayer for Friends' John contrasts his own frailty with his desire to pray for others:

> My good Lord, your servant longs to pray to you for his friends, but your debtor is held back by his faults. For I am not able to pray for my own pardon; with what forwardness may I presume to ask for your grace for others?

53. Rom 7:19.

54. Augustine, *Confessions*, 2.6.7; trans. Chadwick, *Confessions*, 6. Aelred's debt to Augustine is well known, having been first recorded by Walter Daniel in Vita A 42, 51; CF 57:128, 135, and then by such twentieth-century scholars as Squire, *Aelred of Rievaulx*, 37–40, and Courcelle, 'Ailred de Rievaulx', 163–174.

55. Although Augustine's *Confessions* is voiced as a prayer, its length identifies it as having an intellectual rather than a contemplative purpose. Peter Brown describes the work as 'a prolonged exploration of the nature of God, written in the form of a prayer' (*Augustine of Hippo*, 166); Karl Morrison has called it 'a literary genre masquerading as a prayer' ('The End').

56. Ward, Introduction, Anselm, *Prayers and Meditations*, 50, 51–52. Rachel Fulton credits Anselm with stimulating the new christian affectivity of the eleventh and twelfth centuries (*From Judgment to Passion*, 114–186).

And with what boldness shall I, who anxiously seek intercessors, intercede for others? What shall I do, Lord God, what shall I do?[57]

In 'Prayer of a Bishop or an Abbot to the Saint under whose Name he Rules the Church', Anselm expresses his concern for his people in similar language:

> This sinner, this needy one, this one of yours, although unworthy, although inept, too unfitting a vicar, again and again returns to you, doubtful, ignorant, anxious about your people, about your community, and about his own danger.

Again he writes of the contrast between the world's view of him and his own self-awareness: 'I am called master, but I do not know how to be one; I am named pastor, and I do not manage to be so. I am said to be an abbot, but I am not.'[58]

As Aelred reflects on Benedict's requirements for abbots and struggles to write the lived reality of the difficulty of that role, he finds verbal and stylistic help in these prayers. His confession of his love for his monks and of his inadequacy to be their abbot echoes John's and Anselm's words and mirrors their form. Although the pervasive influence of these works means that Aelred's work is less autobiographically transparent than has often been thought, it remains a powerful window into his view of the abbot's role. In *Prayer* Aelred adds his own voice and spiritual longing to this profound tradition of Christian candor and humility while

---

57. John of Fécamp, 'Oratio pro amicis', in Schmitt, *S. Anselmi Opera*, 3:71–72, here 72; in Anselm, *Prayers and Meditations*, 212–215, here 213. Wilmart has identified this prayer, long treated as the eighteenth of Anselm's prayers and meditations, as being by John; see Wilmart, 'L'Oraison', 265 n. 2; rpt. Dumont, *La Prière*, 182.

58. 'Oratio episcopi vel abbatis ad sanctum sub cuius homine regit ecclesiam', Schmitt, *S. Anselmi Opera*, 3:68–70; Anselm, *Prayers*, 201. Wilmart says that in *Prayer* 'one can read distinct echoes of [Anselm's prayer by a bishop] . . . that page was without a doubt familiar to the abbot of Rievaulx, and, naturally, he picked up several terms' ('L'Oraison', 265 n. 2).

also conveying an irresistible sense of his own efforts, hopes, and love for God and for his monks. Powerfully written in the new genre popularized by John and Anselm, *Prayer* reveals personal conviction with every word, embodying Aelred's profound relationship with Jesus and his desire for Jesus' help in the work Jesus has chosen him to do.

EVERYONE A SHEPHERD

Prayer speaks most directly to those who are called to be shepherds, those required by their vocation to love and serve others, to give themselves to the community. In the course of the work Aelred teaches that the essence of the task is not authority, knowledge, skill, study, or even prayer, but love of God and of those God has given to be loved. Moreover, through *Prayer* Aelred's echoing phrases reveal the truth that the person who desires to love loves already. All shepherds may recognize themselves in and learn about themselves from this mirror of self-awareness, of love, of service, and of devotion to Jesus and to Jesus' people.

Although the abbot's vocation dominates *Prayer,* and the fourteenth-century annotator of the work insists that it is intended especially for prelates, the work also speaks with power and meaning to those who are neither monastic superiors nor priests. It reminds readers that they are not alone in their sense of inadequacy or in their failure to pray sufficiently or to listen often to God. The self-appraisal that dominates the work reflects the self-knowledge not only of an abbot but of all who are honest about themselves, their shortcomings, their desire to do and be more than they naturally can—their inability to reach perfection. It allows all to find in Aelred's words not only their truest but also their best-hidden selves.

Aelred thus invites all readers to join in confessing the reality of their own lives, to face themselves and say aloud, 'I have sinned in my thoughts and in my deeds, in what I have done and in what I have failed to do. I have not loved God with my whole heart or my neighbor as myself. There is no health in me.' These are the thoughts and words of Moses and Solomon, Isaiah and Ezekiel, Hagar, Elizabeth, and Mary as surely as they are those of Augustine, John of Fécamp, Anselm, and Aelred. They are the thoughts of every honest man and woman.

Yet despite the imperfection that plagues all human beings, Aelred insists that God calls each one to serve and love, to guide and rule, to pray and teach. Aelred never suggests that he sought to be an abbot or that his community elected him, but declares rather that Jesus chose him for the task and that Jesus will help him fulfill it. He therefore tacitly reassures those who read his words that all people, however flawed and frail and fearful, can serve God and one another. For God surely hears what each reader of Aelred's prayer hears: that the one who seeks to answer God's call already answers and obeys; for the heartfelt desire to be a good shepherd is what God requires of a good shepherd.

In all his works Aelred insists that all people are responsible for the needs of others. In *Spiritual Friendship* he shows such mutual obligation to be part of God's plan in creation, with God placing his own unity within Adam and Eve in order 'that peace should guide all his creatures and society unite them.'[59] In the *Life of Saint Edward,* the king heals his suffering subjects on behalf of God:'Who am I that I should be sad and not rather rejoice if by my hands, however unworthy, the divine loving-kindness can bring the poor man the favor that has been promised him?'[60]

So in *Prayer* Aelred shoulders the role of shepherding the people, praying that as abbot he may keep his community through love and wisdom, both guiding and serving its members, teaching them and expending himself for them. Those who are neither abbots nor abbesses need no great metaphorical leap to understand that they too must love and keep their neighbors. For the responsibility to care for one another, to be Jesus' representative in the monastery of the world, rests with all descendants of Adam and Eve.

59. Spir amic 1.53; CCCM 1:298; CF 5:62.
60. Vita E 22; PL 184:764; CF 57:186.

Prayer thus concerns even those who do not usually think of themselves as shepherds of God's sheep. It teaches that all men and women are to be more loving than they naturally are to all those with whom they live and work. While not all publicly exercise responsibility over others and not all are superiors of the communities in which they live, all men and women are their brothers' and sisters' keepers, for all are members of a single family, of whom Jesus is the father and head.

This family, Aelred says, is composed of those Jesus has gathered to dwell together in a common way of life. Like the members of the early church, they are united in heart and mind and so are responsible for one another—called to be shepherds to one other. Aelred prays not only that he may serve them but that they may serve one another and that the Holy Spirit will dwell in them, to cleanse them and to assist them in caring for and serving one another:

> Pour your Holy Spirit into their hearts to keep them in the unity of the Spirit and the bond of peace, in chastity of flesh and humility of mind. . . . Sweet Lord, by the action of your Spirit may they be peaceful, modest, and kind in their relationships with themselves, with each other, and with me. May they be obedient to one another, of service to one another, and encouraging to one another. (§8)

Serving as a mirror of both humility and charity, *Prayer* offers a portrait of christian responsibility to all whom God has created and gathered together. This theme, a favorite of Aelred's, is a universal one: All are called to guide and protect one another, to love their neighbor as themselves. Aelred's confession of his own lack of preparation properly to love and guide and teach and pray is the confession of each person who desires to care for others— friends, lovers, colleagues, children, students, members of any monastic or parish community. Although Aelred writes out of his own experience and his own particular need, his words allow all readers to recognize in this abbot's concerns their own.

As in defining the intertwined roles of the abbot Benedict relies on the duality of *rego* and of God's repeated address to the kings of Judah as shepherds of his sheep, those reading *Prayer* may benefit from knowledge of an English word of similarly double meaning. From Aelred's time until at least the end of the nineteenth century, *sheep*—a noun as familiar to Aelred as *rego*—could mean either 'sheep' or 'shepherd'. So the great fourteenth-century poem *Piers Plowman* begins with the dreamer-narrator saying 'I shoop me . . . as I a sheep weere'—'I clothed myself as though I were a sheep' or, perhaps, 'a shepherd'.[61] As the author of this poem implies, and as Aelred's *Prayer* reveals, all people are both the sheep of Jesus' pasture and shepherds to his sheep—to love, serve, and give themselves for each member of his people, in imitation of their lord.

---

61. *Piers Plowman*, Prol.2; Kane and Donaldson, eds., *Piers Plowman,* 227.

This volume contains my new critical edition of Aelred's *Pastoral Prayer* and Mark DelCogliano's translation of the edited text, both of which first appeared in *Cistercian Studies Quarterly.*[62] Since 1925 André Wilmart's edition has been repeatedly corrected, altered, reprinted, and translated; the 1971 version published by Anselm Hoste and C. H. Talbot in Corpus Christianorum, Continuatio Mediaevalis 1, departs in several ways from both the manuscript readings and Wilmart's corrected text of 1932. The edition in this volume is the first since Wilmart's to rely entirely on the manuscript.

This edition is conservative, emending only in a few cases of grammatical necessity and retaining manuscript orthography and, except for proper names, capitalization. I have tried to observe the scribe's syntactic indications, even when they result in extremely long sentences, but within sentences I have followed modern conventions of syntactic punctuation. As Jesus MS Q.B. 17 is the sole surviving witness to Aelred's intentions for *Oratio,* I follow its readings whenever possible, inclining always in the direction of obedience rather than contradiction. Thus although in the first sentence I have emended *omnium* to *ouium* because of the following feminine pronoun *tuarum,* I retain *At* in the second sentence rather than emending to *Ad,* allowing for the predictable medieval Latin orthographic variant of *t* for *d.* Such decisions are in part a conscious reaction against Wilmart's occasional stylistic emendations—e.g., the insertion of *et* and *mea* in §7 to enhance parallelism.[63] For ease of reference I follow Wilmart's sectional divisions in both the edition and the translation. I have also provided addi-

---

62. Dutton, ed., 'Oratio Pastoralis'; DelCogliano, trans., 'Oratio Pastoralis'. Both the edition and the translation have undergone minor alterations in this volume.

63. Regarding the insertion of *et* he writes 'I add the copula myself for the parallelism of the phrases' ('L'Oraison', 271 n. 116). A few lines later he adds *mea* without a note, also apparently to enhance parallelism. Hoste and Talbot print both words in angle brackets (nn. 18 and 20 in the edition below).

tional subdivisions, often distinct from those of Dumont or of Hoste and Talbot.

Because *Oratio* survives in a single Rievaulx manuscript of historical importance and because of the scarcity of errors in the text, it seems probable that it was copied and corrected directly from Aelred's holograph. I therefore record corrections made above the line (*sup. lin.*) or in the margin (*in marg.*) of the manuscript, as they may represent readings from the archetype. Two hands are responsible for all corrections. The first hand (R^1) is contemporary and perhaps identical to the scribe's; Wilmart dated the second (R^2) to the thirteenth century.

The textual apparatus notes scribal corrections and marginal insertions in the manuscript and reports the ways in which this text differs from the readings of the manuscript (*R*) and of Hoste and Talbot's 1971 CCCM version (*c*). The apparatus ignores Wilmart's 1925 edition and all adaptations before 1971. The abbreviation *add.* indicates words added by R^1, R^2, or the CCCM editors; *add. sed del.* indicates words that were added and then deleted in the manuscript. The abbreviation *om.* indicates letters and words missing from *R* or *c*. I indicate my own emendations with the word *emendaui*. Vertical lines in the text signal folio references, specified in the footnotes. Italics in the translation and edition indicate direct quotations from the Bible or from the *Rule of Benedict*.

Marsha L. Dutton

Ohio University

THE PRAYER OF VENERABLE AELRED, ABBOT OF RIEVAULX,

MEANT FOR PRELATES AND ESPECIALLY ABBOTS

COMPOSED AND USED BY HIM

INCIPIT ORATIO PASTORALIS

1. O *Bone pastor* Iesu, pastor bone, pastor clemens, pastor pie, ad te clamat miser et miserabilis quidam pastor, et si infirmus, et si inperitus, et si inutilis, ouium[1] tamen tuarum qualiscumque pastor. At[2] te, inquam, clamat, o bone pastor, iste non bonus pastor; ad te clamat, anxius pro se, anxius pro ouibus tuis.

2. Recogitans enim *pristinos annos meos in amaritudine anime mee*, pauesco et contremisco ad nomen pastoris, cui me indignissimum, si non sentio, certe desipio. Sed et si misericordia tua facta[3] est super me ut erueres de inferno inferiori miseram animam meam, qui misereris cui uolueris et misericordiam prestas in quem tibi placuerit, ita peccata condonans, ut nec dampnes ulciscendo, nec confundas inproperando, nec minus diligas inputando, nichilominus tamen confundor et conturbor, memor quidem bonitatis tue, sed non inmemor ingratitudinis mee.

Ecce enim, ecce est ante te confessio cordis mei, confessio innumerabilium criminum meorum, a quorum dominatu sicut placuit

---

1. ouium] *emendaui,* omnium R
2. At] Ad *c*
3. facta] sancta *c*

HERE BEGINS THE PRAYER OF SHEPHERDS

1. O GOOD SHEPHERD Jesus![1] Good shepherd, merciful shepherd, loving shepherd,[2] to you a shepherd now cries, a poor and pitiable shepherd.[3] Though without strength, though without skill or experience, though without anything at all to offer,[4] he is nevertheless the shepherd of your sheep, such as he is.[5] To you, I say, O good shepherd, he cries, this no-good shepherd. To you he cries, worried about himself, worried about your sheep.[6]

2. For when I reflect upon *my earlier years in the bitterness of my soul*,[7] I tremble and shake at the name *shepherd*. Were I unaware of my utter unworthiness, I would certainly be out of my mind. But your mercy came upon me so you could rescue my poor soul from the depths,[8] you who have mercy on whom you will and have compassion on whom it pleases you.[9] You thus pardon our sins that you may not condemn us in vengeance, may not shame us with guilt, may not love us less in chastising us. Nevertheless I am still ashamed and dismayed, mindful of your goodness but not unmindful of my ingratitude.

For here, here before you is the confession of my heart, the confession of my innumerable sins, from whose tyranny you have

---

1. Cf. Jn 10:11–14
2. Cf. *Salve Regina*
3. Cf. John of Fécamp, 'Prayer for Friends', ll. 17–19
4. Cf. Anselm, 'Prayer of a Bishop or Abbot', ll. 5–6
5. Cf. Jn 10:14; cf. Jn 21:17
6. Cf. Ps 101:1 [Vlg]; cf. Anselm, 'Prayer of a Bishop or Abbot', ll. 7, 11–12
7. Is 38:15; Heb 10:32; cf. Augustine, *Confessions* 2.1
8. Cf. Ps 86 [85]:13; cf. Aelred, Inst incl 32
9. Cf. Ex 33:19, cf. Rom 9:15

misericordie tue liberasti infelicem animam meam. Pro quibus omnibus, quantum conari possunt, grates et laudes exsoluunt tibi omnia uiscera mea. Sed non minus debitor tibi sum etiam et pro illis malis quecumque non feci, quoniam certe quicquid mali non feci, te utique gubernante non feci, cum uel subtraheres facultatem, uel uoluntatem corrigeres, uel resistendi dares uirtutem.[4]

Sed quid faciam, Domine Deus meus, et pro hiis quibus adhuc, iusto iudicio tuo, aut fatigari aut prosterni pateris *seruum tuum, filium ancille tue*? Innumerabilia enim sunt, Domine, pro quibus sollicita est in oculis tuis peccatrix anima mea, quamuis non ea contricione, nec tanta cautione, quantam exigeret necessitas mea uel affectaret uoluntas mea.

3. Confiteor itaque tibi, Iesus[5] meus, saluator meus, spes mea,[6] consolatio mea; tibi confiteor, Deus meus, me nec pro preteritis esse adeo contritum uel timidum ut deberem, nec pro presentibus adeo sollicitum ut oporteret. Et tu, dulcis Domine, talem, talem[7] constituisti *super familiam tuam*, super oues *pascue tue*. Et qui parum sollicitus sum pro me ipso, iubes ut sollicitus sim pro illis, et qui pro meis peccatis, meis,[8] orare nequaquam sufficio, iubes me orare pro illis, et qui me ipsum parum docui, iubes ut doceam illos. Miser ego: quid feci, quid presumpsi, quid consensi?

Immo tu, dulcis Domine, quid de hoc misero consensisti? Obsecro, dulcis Domine, nonne hec est familia tua, populus tuus peculiaris,

4. uel resistendi dares uirtutem] *R*[2] *in marg.*
5. Iesus] *emendaui,* iesu *R*
6. spes mea] *R*[2] *sup. lin.*
7. talem talem] talem *c*
8. meis] *om. c*

delivered my unhappy soul as it has pleased your mercy. However much I can, I will pay you back for all this with thanks and praise from the very depths of my being.[10] But I am no less a debtor to you even for those evils that I did not do, because there is no doubt that whatever evil I did not do, I did not do it because you were surely at the helm. You either removed the means I had to do it or rectified the intention I had to do it or gave me the strength to resist it.

But what should I do, O Lord my God, about the things, justly allowed by your judgment, that still fatigue and lay low *your servant, the son of your handmaid*?[11] How countless, O Lord, are the many things my sinful soul is worried about in your eyes! No matter how much contrition, no matter how much caution—all falls short of what my predicament demands and what my will desires.

3. And so I confess to you, my Jesus, my saviour, my hope, my consolation; to you I confess, my God, that I am not so repentant or fearful as I ought to be about what I have done, nor am I so concerned as I should be about what I am now doing. And you, sweet Lord, you have appointed such a one, such a one to be over your family,[12] over the sheep *of your pasture*.[13] Though I have far too little concern for myself, you bid me to be concerned for others; though in every way I lack what it takes to pray for my sins, my own sins, you bid me pray for others; though I myself am far too untaught, you bid me teach others. Wretched me! What have I done? What have I undertaken? What have I agreed to?[14]

Then again, sweet Lord, why have you agreed to this wretch?[15] I beg you to tell me this, sweet Lord: is this not your family,[16] *your*

---

10. Cf. Jr 31:20
11. Cf. Ps 116 [115]:16; cf. Lk 1:38; cf. Ws 9:5
12. Cf. Lk 12:42; cf Mt 24:45
13. Cf. Ps 74 [73]:1; cf. Ps 79 [78]:13
14. Cf. Anselm, 'Prayer of a Bishop or Abbot', ll. 18–20
15. Cf. Anselm, 'Prayer of a Bishop or Abbot', ll. 21–22
16. Cf. Lk 12:42; cf. Mt 24:45

quem secundo eduxisti de Egipto, quem creasti, quem redemisti? Denique de regionibus congregasti eos et habitare facis unius moris in domo.

Cur ergo, fons misericordie, tales tali, tam caros tibi, tam proiecto ab oculis tuis commendare uoluisti? An ut responderes affectionibus meis et traderes me desideriis meis, essemque quem arcius accusares, districtius dampnares, nec pro meis tantum peccatis sed etiam pro alienis punires? | [9] Itane, o piissime, ut esset causa manifestior cur unus peccator acrius puniretur, dignum fuit ut tot et tales periculo exponerentur? Quod enim maius periculum subditis quam stultus prelatus et peccator?[10]

An, quod de tanta bonitate dignius creditur, suauius experitur, ideo talem constituisti super familiam tuam, ut manifesta fieret misericordia tua et notam faceres sapientiam tuam, ut *sublimitas sit uirtutis* tue, non ex homine, ut si forte placuerit benignitati tue per talem bene regere familiam tuam, *non glorietur sapiens in sapientia sua, nec iustus in iusticia sua, nec fortis in fortitudine sua,* quoniam cum bene regunt populum tuum illi, tu pocius regis quam illi? Sic, sic, *non nobis, Domine, non nobis, sed nomini tuo da gloriam.*

9. f. 97^v
10. peccator] *emendaui,* peccor R

42

own people,[17] whom you led out of Egypt[18] for a second time,[19] whom you created, whom you redeemed?[20] At long last you have gathered them from various lands[21] and given those of like mind a home to live in.[22]

Why, then, font of mercy, why would you want to entrust such people, so dear to you, to someone cast so far from your eyes?[23] Was it so that you might acknowledge my inclinations and deliver me up to my desires,[24] that I might be someone whom you could accuse so severely and condemn so sternly, whom you could punish not only for my own sins but also for those of others?[25] If you were going to make it so evident why one sinner was punished so severely, was it really appropriate, O most loving one, that so many of your people, and such people, should be exposed to danger? For what is more dangerous to subordinates than a stupid and sinful superior?

Or, as is much more worthily believed and sweetly experienced of your great goodness, did you appoint such a one as me over your family[26] to manifest your mercy and make your wisdom known?[27] To reveal *excellence as proper to* your *power* and not of human origin?[28] Or perhaps it pleased your graciousness to have someone like me guide your family well, that I might *not glory like the wise in their own wisdom,* or like the just in their own justice, or like *the strong in their own strength*?[29] For when such as these guide your people well, is it not you who guide rather than they? Yes, yes, *not to us, Lord, not to us, but to your name give the glory.*[30]

---

17. Cf. Dt 7:6; cf. Ps 81 [80]:11
18. Cf. Ps 81 [80]:10
19. Cf. Aelred, SS 6.5 (Nat Ben) and 8.2 (Nat Ben); cf. Bernard, S Div 11.3
20. Cf. Ps 107 [106]:2
21. Ps 105:27 [106:28]; cf. Ps 107:3 [106:2]; cf. Jr 23:3; cf. Aelred, S 1.33 (Adv Dom)
22. Cf. Ps 68:6 [67:7]

23. Cf. Ps 31:22 [30:23]
24. Cf. Rom 1:24
25. Cf. Ps 18:14 [Vlg]
26. Cf. Lk 12:42; cf. Mt 24:45
27. Cf. Ps 106 [105]:8
28. Cf. 2 Cor 4:7
29. Jr 9:23
30. Ps 115:1 [113:9]; cf. RB Prol.30; cf. Aelred, Spec car Ep.5

4. Uerum qualicumque iuditio me indignum et peccatorem in hoc officio posuisti, uel poni permisisti, quandiu tamen pateris me preesse illis, iubes me sollicitum esse pro illis et attentius orare pro illis. Ergo, Domine, non *in iustificationibus* meis prosterno *preces ante faciem tuam, sed in miserationibus tuis multis*, et ubi tacet meritum, clamat officium. Sint igitur oculi tui super me et aures tue ad preces meas. Sed quoniam, ut sanxit lex diuina, officium sacerdotis est pro se primo,[11] deinde pro populo sacrificium offerre, qualecumque hoc orationis sacrificium pro peccatis meis primum tue immolo maiestati.

5. Ecce uulnera anime mee, Domine.[12] *Omnia uidet oculus* tuus *uiuus et efficax, et pertingens usque ad diuisionem anime et spiritus.* Uides certe, Domine mi, uides in anima mea et preteritorum peccatorum meorum uestigia et presentium pericula, causas etiam et materias futurorum. Uides hec, Domine, et sic uolo ut uideas. Tu enim scis, o *inspector cordis* mei, quia nichil est in anima mea quod uellem latere oculos tuos, etiam si eorum possem cauere conspectum.

Ue illis quorum uoluntas est ut abscondantur a te! Non enim efficiunt ut non uideantur a te, sed potius ut non sanentur et puniantur a te. Uide me, dulcis Domine; uide me. Spero enim in pietate tua, o misericordissime, quia aut pius medicus uidebis ut sanes. Aut benignissimus magister ut corrigas. Aut indulgentissimus pater ut ignoscas.

---

11. primo] *add. sed del.* orare *R, add.* [orare] *c*
12. Domine] *R*² *sup. lin.*

4. For some good reason you have placed me—or rather let me be placed—in this office, unworthy sinner that I am.[31] For as long as you suffer me to be over your people,[32] you bid me to be concerned for them and to pray so conscientiously for them. Therefore, Lord, it is *not on the basis of my righteousness that I prostrate myself in prayer before your face, but rather on the basis of your great mercy;*[33] for when merit is silent, the duty of office cries out. Therefore set your eyes upon me and turn your ears to my prayers.[34] Because divine law has laid down that it is the priest's duty to offer sacrifice for himself first and then for the people, I will first offer your majesty this sacrifice of prayer, such as it is, for my sins.[35]

5. See the wounds of my soul, Lord! Your *eye, alive and keen, sees everything, even penetrating all the way to the division of soul and spirit.*[36] You certainly see, my Lord, you see in my soul the residue of my past sins and the imminent dangers of my present sins and even the causes and the content of my future sins. You see these, Lord, and that is exactly what I want you to see. For you know, O you who *ponder* my *heart*,[37] that there is nothing in my soul that I would want to conceal from your eyes, even if I could keep such things from your sight.

Woe to those whose will it is to be hidden from you![38] For that makes them not unseen by you but rather unhealed and unpunished by you. Look upon me, sweet Lord, look upon me! I place all my hope in your loving tenderness, O most merciful, because I know that you will look upon me either as a loving physician who will heal me[39] or as a most kind teacher who will set me straight or as a most indulgent father who will pardon me.

---

31. Cf. Anselm, 'Prayer of a Bishop or Abbot', l. 21
32. Cf. RB 64.8
33. Dn 9:18; cf. John of Fécamp, 'Prayer for Friends', ll. 39–40
34. Cf. Ps 34:15 [33:16]
35. Cf. Lv 9:7; cf. Heb 5:3
36. Si 23:27; Heb 4:12
37. Cf. Prv 24:12
38. Cf. Is 29:15
39. Cf. Aelred, Spec car 1.29.84; cf. Aelred, Iesu 1.3; cf. Aelred, SS 32.1 (Pur) and 82.1–2 (Fest Ben)

Hoc est igitur quod rogo, o fons pietatis, confidens de illa omnipotentissima misericordia tua et misericordissima omnipotentia tua, ut in uirtute suauissimi nominis tui et misterii sacrosancte humanitatis tue, dimittas michi peccata mea et sanes languores anime mee, memor bonitatis tue, inmemor ingratitudinis mee; et contra uitia et passiones malas que adhuc inpugnant eam—siue ex antiqua consuetudine mea pessima, siue ex cotidianis et infinitis negligentiis meis, siue ex infirmitate corrupte et uitiate nature mee, siue ex occulta malignorum spirituum temptatione—uirtutem et fortitudinem administret michi dulcis gratia tua, ut non consentiam neque regnent[13] in meo mortali corpore, neque prebeam eis *membra* mea *arma iniquitatis* |[14] donec perfecte sanes infirmitates meas et cures uulnera mea et deformia mea formes.

Descendat Spiritus tuus bonus et dulcis in cor meum et preparet in eo habitaculum sibi, mundans illud *ab omni inquinamento carnis et spiritus*, et infundens ei fidei, spei, et caritatis augmentum, conpunctionis, pietatis, et humanitatis affectum; estus concupiscentiarum rore sue benedictionis extinguat; libidinosas conmotiones et carnales affectiones sua uirtute mortificet. Prestet michi in laboribus, in uigiliis, in abstinentia feruorem et discretionem ad te amandum, laudandum, orandum, meditandum, et omnem secundum te actum et cogitatum, deuotionem et efficaciam, et in hiis omnibus usque ad finem uite mee perseuerantiam.

6. Et hec quidem necessaria michi sunt propter me, o spes mea. Sunt alia quibus indigeo non solum propter me, sed et pro illis quibus me iubes *prodesse magis quam preesse*.[15] Postulauit aliquando

---

13. regnent] *emendaui*, regnet *R*
14. f. 98[r]
15. magis . . . preesse] *R*[1 in marg.]

This, then, is what I ask, O font of loving tenderness,[40] trusting in your most almighty mercy and your most merciful might: that in the power of your name, that sweetest of names, and by the power of the mystery of your sacred humanity, you forgive my sins and heal the feebleness of my soul, remembering your goodness but not remembering my ingratitude. Faults and malicious passions still attack my soul, whether because of my long-standing and terrible habits, or because of my daily and uncountable lapses, or because of the weakness of my corrupt and flawed nature, or because of the surreptitious tempting of evil-minded spirits. May your sweet grace bestow upon me the strength and fortitude to withstand these faults and malicious passions, that I not acquiesce to them, neither letting them hold sway in my mortal body nor allowing them to use my *members as weapons of wickedness*,[41] until you complete the healing of my infirmities, the binding up of my wounds, and the reforming of my deformities.

Let your good and sweet Spirit descend into my heart[42] and prepare in it a dwelling place for himself, cleansing it *from all defilement of flesh and spirit*[43] and pouring into it an increase of *faith, hope, and love*[44] and a disposition of compunction, loving tenderness, and kindness. Let him quench the fire of my cravings with his blessed dew and by his power snuff out my lustful urges and carnal desires.[45] As I labor, keep vigil, and fast, let him bestow upon me the fervor and discernment to love and praise you, to pray to you and meditate on you, the dedication and capability to have all my thoughts and deeds be in harmony with you, and perseverance in all these things until the very end of my life.

6. Now I certainly need all these things for myself because of who I am, O my hope. There are other things that I need not only because of who I am but also because of those you bid me *to profit*

---

40. Cf. John of Fécamp, 'Prayer for Friends', l. 41
41. Cf. Rom 6:12–13
42. Cf. Ps 143 [142]:10; Si 24:27

43. 2 Cor 7:1
44. Cf. 1 Cor 13:13
45. John of Fécamp, 'Prayer for Friends', ll. 39–40

quidam antiquorum sapientiam dari sibi, ut sciret regere populum tuum, rex enim erat, et placuit sermo in oculis tuis et exaudisti uocem eius, et necdum in cruce obieras, necdum illam miram caritatem ostenderas populo tuo.

Ecce, dulcis Domine, ecce in conspectu tuo populus tuus peculiaris, ante quorum oculos crux tua et signa passionis tue in eis. Hos regendos conmisisti huic peccatori seruulo tuo. Deus meus, tu scis insipientiam meam, et infirmitas mea a te non est abscondita. Peto itaque, dulcis Domine, non aurum, non argentum, non lapides presciosos dari michi, sed sapientiam, ut sciam regere populum tuum. Emitte eam, o fons sapientie, de *sede magnitudinis tue ut mecum sit, mecum laboret,* mecum operetur, in me loquatur, disponat cogitationes, sermones, et omnia opera mea et consilia mea, secundum bonum placitum[16] tuum, ad honorem nominis tui, ad eorum profectum et meam salutem.

7. Tu scis, Domine, cor meum: quia quicquid dederis seruo tuo, uoluntas mea est ut totum inpendatur illis et totum expendatur pro illis, insuper et ipse libenter inpendar[17] pro illis. Sic fiat, Domine mi; sic fiat. Sensus meus,[18] sermo meus,[19] ocium meum et occupatio mea, actus meus et cogitatio mea, prosperitas mea et aduersitas mea, mors mea et uita mea, sanitas[20] et infirmitas mea—quicquid omnino sum, quod uiuo, quod sentio, quod discerno—totum inpendatur illis et totum expendatur pro illis, pro quibus tu ipse non dedignabaris expendi.

---

16. bonum placitum] beneplacitum *c*
17. inpendar] impendat *c*
18. meus] *add.* <et> *c*
19. sermo meus] *R*[1 in marg.]
20. sanitas] *add.* <mea> *c*

rather than to preside over.[46] One of the men of old once begged to be given wisdom so that he might know how to guide your people.[47] He was a king, and his request found pleasure in your eyes; you listened to his voice, even though it was before you died on the cross, even though it was before you displayed that wonderful act of love to your people.

Here, sweet Lord, here in your sight are your own people. Before their eyes are your cross and the signs of your passion. You have entrusted them to this sinner, your trifling servant, for guidance. My God, you are well aware of my stupidity, and my weakness is not hidden from you.[48] And so, sweet Lord, I ask to be given not gold or silver or jewels, but rather wisdom so that I may know how to guide your people. O *font of wisdom,*[49] send her forth *from the throne of your glory so that she may be with me, toil with me,* work with me, speak in me, and bring my thoughts and my words, all my undertakings and decisions,[50] into harmony with your good will, to the honor of your name, for their progress and my salvation.

7. You know my heart, O Lord: whatever you have given to your servant, it is my will that it be expended upon them in its entirety and entirely spent on them. Still more, may I find happiness in being utterly spent for them.[51] Let it be done in this way, my Lord, let it be done in this way! All my feeling, all my speaking, all my rest and all my work, all my action and all my thought, all my success and all my hardship, all my death and all my life, all my health and sickness—all that I am, all that gives me life, all that I feel, all that I discern[52]—let all this be expended upon them in all its entirety and entirely spent for their benefit, for the benefit of those for whom you yourself did not consider it unworthy to be utterly spent.[53]

---

46. RB 64.8; cf. Ws 9:1–12; cf. Aelred, Vita E Prol
47. 2 Chr 1:7–12; 1 [3] K 3:5–9
48. Cf. Ps 69:5 [68:6]
49. Prv 18:4
50. Ws 9:10–11
51. Cf. 2 Cor 12:15
52. cf. Aelred, Oner 15.1; cf. William of Saint Thierry, Med 3.3
53. Cf. Walter Daniel, Vita A 27

Doce me itaque seruum tuum, Domine; doce me, queso, per Spiritum sanctum tuum, quomodo me inpendam illis et quomodo me expendam pro illis. Da michi, Domine, per ineffabilem gratiam tuam, ut patienter sustineam infirmitates eorum, pie conpaciar, discrete subueniam. Discam magisterio spiritus tui mestos consolari, pusillanimes roborare, lapsos erigere, infirmari cum infirmis, uri cum scandalizatis, omnibus omnia fieri, ut omnes lucrifaciam. Da uerum sermonem et rectum[21] et bene sonantem in os meum, quo edificentur in fide, spe, et caritate, in castitate et humilitate, in pacientia et obedientia, in spiritus feruore et mentis deuotione.

Et quoniam | [22] tu dedisti illis hunc cecum ductorem, indoctum doctorem, nescium rectorem, et si non propter me, propter illos tamen doce quem doctorem posuisti, duc quem alios ducere precepisti, rege quem rectorem statuisti. Doce me itaque, dulcis Domine, corripere inquietos, consolari pusillanimes, suscipere infirmos, et unicuique pro natura, pro moribus, pro affectione, pro capacitate, pro simplicitate, pro loco et tempore, sicut tu uideris expedire, memetipsum conformare.

Et quoniam—uel *propter infirmitatem carnis* mee, uel propter pusillanimitatem spiritus mei, uel propter uitium cordis mei—parum uel certe nichil edificant eos labor aut uigilie aut abstinentia mea, edificet eos, rogo, largiente misericordia tua, humilitas mea, caritas

21. et rectum] *R¹ in marg.*
22. f. 98ᵛ

O Lord, teach me, your servant; teach me, I beseech you, through your Holy Spirit, how I can spend myself for them and how I can expend myself entirely for them. Through your indescribable grace, O Lord, enable me patiently to support their weaknesses, to have compassion on them lovingly, and discerningly to help them. Let me learn, let your Spirit teach me, to console the sorrowing, to strengthen the fainthearted, to set the fallen upright, to be weak with the weak,[54] to be indignant with the scandalized,[55] to become all things to all people in order to win them all.[56] Grant me a true and upright way of speaking and an eloquence of mouth to build them up in *faith, hope, and love*,[57] in chastity and humility, in patience and obedience, in fervor of spirit and devotion of mind.

And because you have given them this *blind leader*,[58] this untaught teacher,[59] this ignorant guide, teach the one you have put in a teacher's position, lead the one you have commanded to lead others, guide the one you have appointed as a guide[60]—if not for me, then for them! Therefore teach me, sweet Lord, to admonish the disturbed, to console the fainthearted, to support the weak,[61] and *to accommodate* myself *to each one's character*,[62] disposition, inclinations, aptitude, or simplicity, according to the place and time, as seems best to you.[63]

And whereas, either *because of the weakness of* my *flesh*[64] or the faintheartedness of my spirit or the faults of my heart, they are barely, or perhaps not at all, being built up by my efforts or vigils or fasting, I beg you to build them up, through your bountiful mercy, by my humility, my love, my patience, and my mercy. Build

54. Cf. 1 Cor 9:22
55. Cf. 2 Cor 11:29
56. Cf. 1 Cor 9:19–22
57. 1 Cor 13:13; cf. Gilbert of Hoyland, S 6.2
58. Cf. Mt 15:14
59. Cf. Gregory the Great, *Dialogues* 2.1; cf. Prv 14:33; cf. Aelred, Spec car 1.34.100; cf. Aelred, S 56.5 (Fest Ben)
60. Anselm, 'Prayer of a Bishop or Abbot', ll. 24–28
61. Cf. 1 Thes 5:14
62. RB 2.32
63. Cf. Aelred, Oner 28:23–24
64. Rom 6:19; Gal 4:13

mea, patientia mea, et misericordia mea. Edificet illos sermo meus
et doctrina mea, et prosit illis semper oratio mea.

8. Tu autem, misericors Deus noster, *exaudi me* pro illis, quem ad
orandum te pro illis et officium conpellit et inuitat affectus. Animat
autem consideratio tue benignitatis. Tu scis, dulcis Domine, quantum diligam eos, quomodo effusa sint in illos uiscera mea, quomodo liquescat super illos affectus meus. Tu scis, mi Domine, quod
non in[23] austeritate neque in potentia spiritus mei imperem illis,
quomodo optem in caritate *prodesse magis quam preesse* illis, in
humilitate substerni illis. Affectu autem esse in illis quasi unus ex
illis.

Exaudi me itaque; *exaudi me, Domine* Deus meus, *ut sint oculi tui
aperti super* illos *die ac nocte.* Expande piissimas[24] alas tuas et protege
eos; extende dexteram tuam sanctam et benedic eos; infunde in
corda eorum Spiritum tuum sanctum, qui seruet eos *in unitate
spiritus* et *uinculo pacis*, in carnis castitate et mentis humilitate. Ipse
assit orantibus, et adipe et pinguedine dilectionis tue repleat uiscera
eorum, et suauitate compunctionis reficiat mentes eorum, et lu-
mine gratie tue illustret corda eorum, spe erigat, timore humiliet,
caritate inflammet. Ipse eis preces suggerat, quas tu uelis propitius
exaudire.

Ipse dulcis Spiritus tuus insit meditantibus, ut ab eo illuminati
cognoscant te et memorie sue inprimant quem in aduersis inuocent

---

23. in] *om. c*
24. piissimas] piissime *c*

them up by my speaking and my teaching, and let them always derive benefit from my prayers.

8. Our God of mercy, *hear me*[65]—for their sake! I pray to you for their sake, compelled by the duty of my office, urged on by my attachment to them,[66] yet quickened with joy when I contemplate your kindness. You know, sweet Lord, how much I love them, how I have poured out on them all that I can from the depths of my being,[67] how my heart melts over them. You know, my Lord, that I do not order them around harshly or out of an overblown sense of my authority.[68] You know how I want to *profit them* in love *rather than to preside over them*,[69] to be placed in a humble position below them but also to be held in affection among them as one of them.

Hear *me* then*, O Lord* my God, *hear me,*[70] *so that your eyes may watch over* them *day and night.*[71] Spread out your most loving wings and protect them.[72] Stretch out your holy right hand and bless them. Pour your Holy Spirit into their hearts[73] to keep them in *the unity of the Spirit* and *the bond of peace,*[74] in chastity of flesh and humility of mind. Let him be near those who pray. Let him fill their inner depths with the richness and abundance of your love.[75] Let him refresh their minds with the sweetness of sorrow for sin. Let him fill their hearts with the light of your grace. Let him stand them upright with hope, lay them low with reverence, and set them on fire with love. Let your Spirit inspire in them the kind of prayers that you would favorably answer.

Let him, your sweet Spirit, be in those who meditate so that, enlightened by him, they may know you and have their memories

65. Cf. 1 [3] K 18:37
66. Cf. Aelred, Oner 1.10
67. Cf. Jb 16:14
68. Cf. Ez 34:4
69. Cf. RB 64.8; cf. Aelred, Vita E Prol
70. 1 [3] K 18:37
71. 1 [3] K 8:29
72. Cf. Dt 32:11
73. Cistercian Missal, Prayer *Infunde* for General Chapter
74. Cf. Eph 4:3
75. Cf. Ps 63:5 [62:6]; cf. John of Fécamp, 'Prayer for Friends', ll. 43–46

et consulant in dubiis. In temptatione laborantibus ipse pius consolator occurrat et succurrat, et in angustiis et tribulationibus uite huius adiuuet[25] infirmitatem eorum.

Sint, dulcis Domine, ipso Spiritu tuo operante, et in se ipsis et ad inuicem et ad me pacati, modesti, beniuoli, inuicem obedientes, inuicem seruientes et *supportantes inuicem*. Sint *spiritu feruentes, spe gaudentes*, in paupertate, in abstinentia, *in laboribus* et *uigiliis*, in silentio et quiete, per omnia patientes. Repelle ab eis, Domine, spiritum superbie et uane glorie, inuidie et tristicie, accidie et blasphemie, desperationis et diffidentie, fornicationis et inmundicie, presumptionis et discordie.

Esto secundum fidelem promissionem tuam in medio eorum, et quoniam tu scis quid cuique opus est, obsecro ut quod infirmum est | [26] in illis tu consolides, quod debile non proicias, quod morbidum sanes, quod mestum letifices, quod tepidum accendas, quod instabile confirmes, ut singuli in suis necessitatibus et temptationibus tuam sibi gratiam sentiant non deesse.

9. Porro, de his temporalibus quibus in hac uita miseri huius corpusculi sustentatur infirmitas, sicut uideris et uolueris prouide seruis tuis. Hoc unum peto a dulcissima pietate tua, Domine mi, ut quicquid illud fuerit, siue parum, siue multum, facias me, seruum tuum, omnium que dederis fidelem dispensatorem, discretum

25. adiuuet] adiuet *c*
26. f. 99[r]

stamped with your image, the image of the one whom they should call upon in times of adversity and consult in times of doubt. Let him be the tender and loving comfort who races to help them in their struggles with temptation. Let him compensate for their weaknesses when life overwhelms them with anxiety and tribulation.

Sweet Lord, by the action of your Spirit may they be peaceful, modest, and kind in their relationships with themselves, with each other, and with me. May they be obedient to one another,[76] of service to one another,[77] and *encouraging to one another*.[78] May they be *fervent in spirit, joyful in hope*,[79] in poverty, in fasting, *in toils and keeping vigil*,[80] in silence and quiet, and in all things patient.[81] Drive from them, O Lord, the spirit of pride and vainglory, envy and sadness, sloth and slander, despair and indifference, lust and uncleanness, presumption and discord.

Be in the midst of them according to your faithful promise.[82] And because you know what everyone needs, I beseech you: add strength to what is weak in them[83] and do not condemn what is feeble; heal what is diseased, bring joy to what is sorrowful, enkindle what is lukewarm, firm up what is shaky. Then every single one of them will feel that your grace is not lacking to them in their time of need and temptation.

9. Furthermore, provide for your servants those things required in this life to support the weakness of this wretched little body, as seems best to you and as you choose. I beg this one thing of your most tender love, my Lord: no matter what it is, whether it is a little or a lot, make me, your servant, the dependable dispenser,[84] the discerning distributor, the prudent provider of all that you have given. My God, inspire in them as well a willingness to endure in

76. Cf. RB 71.1
77. Cf. RB 35.1
78. Col 3:13
79. Rom 12:11–12
80. 2 Cor 6:5

81. Cf 1 Thes 5:14
82. Cf. Mt 18:20
83. Cf. Ez 34:4
84. Cf. Lk 12:42

distributorem, prudentem prouisorem. Inspira et illis, Deus meus, ut patienter sustineant quando non dederis, moderate utantur quando dederis, et ut de me seruo tuo, et propter te etiam illorum, semper hoc credant et sentiant quod utile sit illis, tantum diligant et timeant me quantum uideris expedire illis.

10. Ego autem conmendo eos sanctis manibus tuis et pie proui-dentie tue, ut non rapiat eos quisquam de manu tua, nec de manu serui tui cui conmendasti eos, sed in sancto proposito feliciter perseuerent. Perseuerantes, autem, uitam eternam optineant, te prestante, dulcissimo Domino nostro, qui uiuis et regnas per omnia secula seculorum. Amen.

patience when you give nothing and to use in moderation when you do give. I am your servant and, because of you, also theirs; grant them the grace to trust me always and to feel that what I am doing is to their advantage. Let them love and respect me as much as you think is beneficial for them.[85]

10. I, however, entrust them into your holy hands and to your loving providence, in the hope that not even one of them will be snatched out of your hand[86] or out of the hand of your servant to whom you have entrusted them, but that they may persevere joyously in their holy intention. By persevering may they obtain everlasting life.[87] Grant this, our sweetest Lord, who live and reign forever and ever. Amen.

85. Cf. RB 64.15; cf. Aelred, Lam D 2
86. Cf. Jn 10:28

87. Cf. John of Fécamp, 'Prayer for Friends', ll. 96–102; cf. RB 73.2, 4

Select Bibliography

EDITIONS AND TRANSLATIONS OF *ORATIO PASTORALIS*

De Briey, Gaétane, trans. 'Prière d'un pasteur'. Aelred of Rievaulx. *Sermons pour l'année, 5.* Pain de Cîteaux, series 3, 24. Oka: Notre-Dame-du-Lac, 2005. 261–270.

De Caluwe, M., trans. 'Aelred van Rievaulx. Gebed van een zieleherder'. *Tijdschrift voor Geestelijk Leven* February 1962: 122–131.

DelCogliano, Mark, trans. 'Aelred of Rievaulx. *Oratio Pastoralis*'. Intro. Marsha L. Dutton. CSQ 37 (2002) 453–459.

Dumont, Charles, trans. 'La prière pastorale' [with Wilmart edition]. *La vie de recluse*[;] *la prière pastorale.* Intro. Anselm Hoste. SCh 76. Paris: Cerf, 1961. 171–203.

Dutton, Marsha L., ed. 'Aelred of Rievaulx's *Oratio Pastoralis*: A New Critical Edition'. CSQ 38 (2003) 297–308.

Friedrich, E. 'Die *Oratio pastoralis* des hl. Aelred'. *Cistercienser Chronik* 51 (1939) 191–195.

Hoste, Anselm, and C. H. Talbot, eds. 'Oratio Pastoralis'. *Aelredi Rievallensis Opera Omnia.* CCCM 1. Turnhout: Brepols Publishers, 1971. 757–763.

Lawson, R. Penelope, trans. *The Pastoral Prayer of St Aelred of Rievaulx* [with Wilmart edition]. Westminster: Dacre, 1955. 25–32. Rpt. 'The Pastoral Prayer'. Aelred of Rievaulx. *Treatises 1.* CF 2. Spencer, MA: Cistercian, 1971. 103–118.

Leyra de Castro, P., trans. 'La Oración Pastoral de san Elredo, abad de Rieval'. Intro. A. Gomez de las Barcenas. *Cistercium* 12 (1960) 172–185.

Miquel, Pierre. *Les moines et la prière.* Paris: Desclée de Brouwer, 1983.

Pezzini, Domenico, trans. 'Preghiera Pastorale'. *Gesù Dodicenne*[;] *Preghiera Pastorale.* Letture Cristiane del Secundo Millennio 29. Milan: Figlie di San Paolo, 2001. 129–151.

Sister Rose de Lima, trans. 'Pastoral Prayer'. *For Crist Luve: Prayers of Saint Aelred Abbot of Rievaulx*. Ed. Anselm Hoste. Steenbrugge: St.-Pietersabdij, 1965. 39–54.

Wilmart, André, ed. 'Le texte de la prière d'Ælred'. RBen 41 (1929) 74.

——. 'L'Oraison pastorale de l'abbé Aelred'. RBen 37 (1925) 263–272. [L'Oraison]

——. 'L'Oraison pastorale de l'abbé Ælred.' *Auteurs spirituels et textes dévots du moyen âge latin*. Paris: Études Augustiniennes, 1932. 287–298. [OP]

EDITIONS AND ENGLISH TRANSLATIONS OF OTHER WORKS BY AELRED OF RIEVAULX

Aelred of Rievaulx. *Aelredi Rievallensis Opera Omnia, 1 Opera Ascetica*. Ed. Anselm Hoste and C. H. Talbot. CCCM 1. Turnhout: Brepols Publishers, 1971.

——. 'Ailredi Abbatis Rievallensis Historia de bello standardii tempore Stephani Regis', 'Genealogia regum Anglorum', 'Vita et miraculis Edwardi Regis et Confessoris', 'De quodam miraculo mirabili'. *Historiæ Anglicanæ Scriptores X*. Ed. Roger Twysden and John Selden. 2 vols. London: Cornelius Bee, 1652. 333–422.

——. 'De bello standardii tempore Stephani regis', 'Genealogia regum Anglorum', 'Vita S. Edwardi regis et confessoris', 'De sanctimoniali de Wattun'. *Beati Aelredi Rievallis abbatis. Operum pars secunda.—Historica*. PL 195:701–796.

——. 'De sancti ecclesiæ Haugustaldensis'. *The Priory of Hexham: Its Chroniclers, Endowments, and Annals*. Ed. James Raine. Surtees Society 44. Durham: Andrews and Co., 1864. 173–203.

——. *Dialogue on the Soul*. Trans. C. H. Talbot. CF 22. Kalamazoo: Cistercian Publications, 1981.

——. *The Historical Works*. Trans. Jane Patricia Freeland. Ed. and Intro. Marsha L. Dutton. CF 56. Kalamazoo: Cistercian Publications, 2005.

——. *Homeliae de oneribus propheticis Isaiae*. Ed. Gaetano Raciti. CCCM 2D. Turnhout: Brepols Publishers, 2005.

——. '*In translacione sancti Edwardi confessoris*: The Lost Sermon by Ælred of Rievaulx Found?' Ed. and intro. Peter Jackson. Trans. Tom License. CSQ 40 (2005) 46–83.

——. 'The Life of Ninian'. Trans. Winifrid MacQueen. *St. Nynia with a Translation of the Miracula Nynie Episcopi and the Vita Niniani*. John MacQueen. Edinburgh: Polygon Books, 1990. 102–133.

———. 'The Life of S. Ninian'. *Lives of S. Ninian and S. Kentigern*. Ed. Alexander Penrose Forbes. Edinburgh: Edmonston and Douglas, 1874. 1–26.

———. *The Liturgical Sermons: The First Clairvaux Collection*. Trans. Theodore Berkeley and M. Basil Pennington. CF 58. Kalamazoo: Cistercian Publications, 2001.

———. *The Lives of the Northern Saints*. Trans. Jane Patricia Freeland. Ed. and Intro. Marsha L. Dutton. CF 71. Kalamazoo: Cistercian Publications, 2006.

———. *Mirror of Charity*. Trans. Elizabeth Connor. Intro. Charles Dumont. CS 17. Kalamazoo: Cistercian Publications, 1990.

———. 'Relatio Venerabilis Aelredi, Abbatis Rievallensis, de Standardo'. *Chronicles of the Reigns of Stephen, Henry II., and Richard I*. Ed. Richard Howlett. 3 vols. Rolls series. London, 1884–1886. 3:lviii–lx, 179–199.

———. *Sermones I–XLVI*. Ed. Gaetano Raciti. CCCM 2A. Turnhout: Brepols Publishers, 1983.

———. *Sermones XLVII–LXXXIV*. Ed. Gaetano Raciti. CCCM 2B. Turnhout: Brepols Publishers, 2001.

———. *Spiritual Friendship*. Trans. Mary Eugenia Laker. CF 5. Kalamazoo: Cistercian Publications, 1977.

———. *Treatises and the Pastoral Prayer*. CF 2. Kalamazoo: Cistercian Publications, 1971.

———. 'Vita Niniani ab Ailredo' and 'Eulogium Davidis ab Ailredo'. *Vitæ Antiquæ Sanctorum qui Habitaverunt in ea parte Britanniæ nunc vocata Scotia vel in ejus insulis*. Ed. Johannes Pinkerton. London: Johannis Nichols, 1789. [xix]–[xx], 1–23, 437–456.

———. 'Vita Niniani', 'Eulogium Davidis ab Ailredo', 'Officium Niniani'. *Pinkerton's Lives of the Scottish Saints*. Ed. W. M. Metcalfe. 2 vols. Paisley: Alexander Gardner, 1889. 1:9–47; 2:269–285.

Other Sources

Anselm of Canterbury. *The Prayers and Meditations of Saint Anselm with the Proslogion*. Trans. and intro. Benedicta Ward. London: Penguin Books, 1973.

———. *S. Anselmi Cantuariensis Archiepiscopi Opera Omnia*. Ed. F. S. Schmitt. 3 vols. Edinburgh: Thomas Nelson and Sons, 1946.

Augustine. *Confessions*. CC 27. Turnhout: Brepols Publishers, 1953.

———. *Confessions*. Trans. Henry Chadwick. Oxford: Oxford University Press, 1991.

Bell, David N. *An Index of Authors and Works in Cistercian Libraries in Great Britain.* CS 130. Kalamazoo: Cistercian Publications, 1992.

———. *The Libraries of the Cistercians, Gilbertines, and Premonstratensians.* Corpus of British Library Catalogues 3. London: The British Library, 1992.

Bernard of Clairvaux. *Sancti Bernardi Opera.* Ed. Jean Leclercq, H. M. Rochais, and C. H. Talbot. 8 vols. Rome: Editiones Cistercienses, 1957–1977.

Boquet, Damien. *L'ordre de l'affect au Moyen Âge: Autour de l'anthropologie affective d'Aelred de Rievaulx.* Caen: Publications de CRAHM, 2005.

Brown, Peter. *Augustine of Hippo: A Biography.* Berkeley: University of California Press, 1967.

Burton, Pierre-André. 'Aux origines de l'expansion anglaise de Cîteaux. La fondation de Rievaulx et la conversion d'Aelred: 1128–1134 (I, II)'. Coll 61 (1999) 186–214, 248–290. Rpt. of part I: 'The Beginnings of Cistercian Expansion in England'. CSQ 42 (2007) 151–182.

———. *Bibliotheca Ælrediana Secunda: Une Bibliographie Cumulative (1962–1996).* Textes et Études du Moyen Âge 7. Louvain-la-Neuve, 1997.

Cassian, Johannes. *Cassiani Opera: Collationes XXIIII.* Ed. Michael Petschenig. CSEL 13. Vienna: Verlag der Österreichischen Akademie der Wissenschaften, 2004.

Chenu, M.–D. 'Theology and the New Awareness of History'. *Nature, Man, and Society in the Twelfth Century.* Trans. Jerome Taylor and Lester K. Little. Chicago: University of Chicago Press, 1968. 162–199.

Courcelle, Pierre. 'Ailred de Rievaulx à l'école des *Confessions*'. *Revue des Études Augustiniennes* 3 (1957) 163–174.

de Vogüé, Adalbert. *La communauté et l'abbé dans la Règle de Saint Benoit.* Paris: Desclée de Brouwer, 1961.

Dumont, Charles. 'Introduction: Aelred of Rievaulx: His Life and Works'. Aelred of Rievaulx. *The Mirror of Charity.* Trans. Elizabeth Connor. CF 17. Kalamazoo: Cistercian Publications, 1990. 11–67.

———. 'L'hymne "Dulcis Jesus memoria": Le "Jubilus" serait-il d'Aelred de Rievaulx?' *S. Aelred de Rievaulx. Le Miroir de la Charité (Journées d'Études— Abbaye de Scourmont 5–9 octobre 1992). Hommage au P. Charles Dumont.* Coll 55 (1993) 233–238.

Du Roy, Olivier. 'Reading RSB Today with Special Reference to the Chapters on the Abbot'. CSQ 6 (1971) 239–248.

Dutton, Marsha L. 'Aelred, Historian: Two Portraits in Plantagenet Myth'. CSQ 28 (1993) 112–143.

———. 'The Cistercian Source: Aelred, Bonaventure, and Ignatius'. *Goad and Nail: Studies in Medieval Cistercian History, X.* Ed. E. Rozanne Elder. CS 84. Kalamazoo: Cistercian, 1985. 151–178.

———. 'The Conversion and Vocation of Aelred of Rievaulx: A Historical Hypothesis'. *England in the Twelfth Century*. Ed. Daniel Williams. London: Boydell, 1990. 31–49.

———. 'Friendship and the Love of God: Augustine's Teaching in the *Confessions* and Aelred of Rievaulx's Response in *Spiritual Friendship*'. ABR 56 (2005) 3–40.

———. 'A Historian's Historian: The Place of Bede in Aelred's Contributions to the New History of his Age.' *Truth as Gift: Studies in Cistercian History in Honor of John R. Sommerfeldt*. Ed. Marsha L. Dutton, Daniel M. La Corte, and Paul Lockey. CS 204. Kalamazoo: Cistercian, 2004. 407–448.

France, James. *The Cistercians in Medieval Art*. Thrupp (UK): Sutton Publishing; Kalamazoo: Cistercian Publications, 1998.

Fry, Timothy, ed. *RB 1980: The Rule of St. Benedict*. Collegeville: The Liturgical Press, 1981.

Fulton, Rachel. *From Judgment to Passion: Devotion to Christ and the Virgin Mary, 800–1200*. New York: Columbia University Press, 2003.

Gregory the Great. *The Book of Pastoral Rule and Selected Epistles*. Library of Nicene and Post-Nicene Fathers of the Christian Church. 2nd series. Trans. James Barmby. Vol. 12b. Edinburgh: T&T Clark, [n.d.]; rpt Grand Rapids: William B. Eerdmans Publishing Company, 1989.

———. *Liber Regulae Pastoralis*. Ed. and trans. H. R. Bramley. Oxford: J. Parker, 1874.

Hoste, Anselm. *Bibliotheca Aelrediana*. Instrumenta Patristica 2. The Hague: Martinus Nijhoff, 1962.

James, Bruno Scott, trans. *The Letters of St Bernard of Clairvaux*. Intro. Beverly Mayne Kienzle. 1953; Kalamazoo: Cistercian Publications, 1998.

James, M. R. *A Descriptive Catalogue of the Manuscripts in the Library of Jesus College, Cambridge*. London: C. J. Clay and Sons, 1895. 43–56.

John of Fécamp. 'Oratio pro amicis'. *S. Anselmi Cantuariensis Archiepiscopi Opera Omnia*. Ed. F. S. Schmitt. Edinburgh: Thomas Nelson and Sons, 1946. 3:71–72.

———. 'Prayer for Friends'. *The Prayers and Meditations of Saint Anselm with the Proslogion*. Trans. and Intro. Benedicta Ward. London: Penguin Books, 1973. 212–215.

Knowles, David. 'The Case of St William of York'. *The Historian and Character*. Cambridge: Cambridge University Press, 1963. 76–97.

Lackner, Bede K. 'The Liturgy of Early Cîteaux'. *Studies in Medieval Cistercian History* [I]. Ed. M. Basil Pennington. CS 13. Shannon: Cistercian Publications, 1971.

La Corte, Daniel M. 'Abbot as *Magister* and *Pater* in the Thought of Bernard of Clairvaux and Aelred of Rievaulx'. *Truth as Gift: Studies in Medieval Cistercian History in Honor of John R. Sommerfeldt*. Ed. Marsha L. Dutton, Daniel M. La Corte, and Paul Lockey. CS 204. Kalamazoo: Cistercian, 2004. 377–405.

———. 'Aelred on Abbatial Responsibilities'. *A Companion to Aelred*. Ed. Marsha L. Dutton. Leiden: Brill Academic Publishers, forthcoming 2009.

La Règle du Maître. Ed. Adalbert de Vogüé. SCh 105. Paris: Les Éditions du Cerf, 1964.

Morrison, Karl. 'The End of Christian Art'. Plenary address, 35th International Medieval Studies Congress, Kalamazoo, Michigan. 5 May 2000.

Obermeier, Anita. *The History and Anatomy of Auctorial Self-Criticism in the European Middle Ages*. Amsterdam and Atlanta: Editions Rodopi B.V., 1999.

Peifer, Claude. 'Appendix 2. The Abbot'. *RB 1980*. Ed. Timothy Fry. Collegeville: The Liturgical Press, 1981. 322–378.

Piers Plowman: The B Version. Ed. George Kane and E. Talbot Donaldson. London: The Athlone Press, 1975.

Quenardel, Olivier. 'Cistercian Diakonia'. CSQ 41 (2006) 443–459.

Reginald of Durham. *De admirandis Beati Cuthberti uirtutibus*. Ed. James Raine. Surtees Society 1. London: J. B. Nichols and Son, 1835.

The Rule of the Master. Trans. Luke Eberle. Kalamazoo: Cistercian Publications, 1977.

Sommerfeldt, John R. *Aelred of Rievaulx: On Love and Order in the World and the Church*. New York: The Newman Press, 2006.

———. *Aelred of Rievaulx: Pursuing Perfect Happiness*. New York: The Newman Press, 2005.

Squire, Aelred. *Aelred of Rievaulx: A Study*. CS 50. 1969; Kalamazoo: Cistercian Publications, 1981.

Stiegman, Emero. '"Woods and Stones" and "The Shade of the Trees" in the Mysticism of Saint Bernard'. *Truth as Gift: Studies in Medieval Cistercian History in Honor of John R. Sommerfeldt*. Ed. Marsha L. Dutton, Daniel M. La Corte, and Paul Lockey. CS 204. Kalamazoo: Cistercian, 2004. 321–354.

Waddell, Chrysogonus. 'Notes toward the Exegesis of a Letter by Saint Stephen Harding'. *Noble Piety and Reformed Monasticism: Studies in Cistercian History VII*. Ed. E. Rozanne Elder. CS 65. Kalamazoo: Cistercian, 1981. ii, 10–39.

———. 'The Origin and Early Evolution of the Cistercian Antiphonary: Reflections on Two Cistercian Chant Reforms'. *The Cistercian Spirit: A*

Symposium in Memory of Thomas Merton. Ed. M. Basil Pennington. CS 3. Kalamazoo: Cistercian Publications, 1979. 190–223.

Walter Daniel. *La vie d'Ælred, abbé de Rievaulx.* Trans. and intro. Pierre-André Burton. Pain de Cîteaux series 3 no. 19. Oka: Abbaye Cistercienne Notre-Dame-du-Lac, 2003.

———. *Vita Ailredi Abbatis Rievall'.* Ed. and trans. F. M. Powicke. 1950; Oxford: Oxford University Press, 1978. Trans. rpt. *The Life of Aelred of Rievaulx and the Letter to Maurice.* Intro. Marsha L. Dutton. CF 57. Kalamazoo: Cistercian Publications, 1994.

Wilmart, André. *Le 'Jubilus' dit de saint Bernard (Étude avec textes).* Edizioni di Storia e Letteratura. Rome, 1944.

Table of Scriptural References

Column one indicates the scriptural reference, and column two identifies the page numbers on which the reference appears in Latin and English in this volume. Vulgate references are in brackets.

Exodus	
33:19	38/39
Leviticus	
9:7	44/45
Deuteronomy	
7:6	40/43
32:11	52/53
1 [3] Kings	
3:5–9	48/49
8:29	52/53
18:37	52/53
2 Chronicles	
1:7–12	48/49
Job	
16:14	52/53
Psalms	
18:14 [Vlg]	42/43
31:22 [30:23]	42/43
34:15 [33:16]	44/45
63:5 [62:6]	52/53

68:6 [67:7]	42/43
69:5 [68:6]	48/49
74 [73]:1	40/41
79 [78]:13	40/41
81 [80]:10	42/43
81 [80]:11	42/43
86 [85]:13	38/39
101:1 [Vlg]	38/39
105:27 [106:28]	42/43
106 [105]:8	42/43
107 [106]:2	42/43
107:3 [106:2]	42/43
115:1 [113:9]	42/43
116 [115]:16	40/41
143 [142]:10	46/47
Proverbs	
14:33	50/51
18:4	48/49
24:12	44/45
Wisdom	
9:1–12	46/46–49
9:5	40/41

9:10–11	48/49	*Romans*	
		1:24	42/43
Sirach (Ecclesiasticus)		6:12–13	46/47
23:27	44/45	6:19	50/51
24:27	46/47	9:15	38/39
		12:11–12	54/55
Isaiah			
29:15	44/45	*1 Corinthians*	
38:15	38/39	9:19–22	50/51
		9:22	50/51
Ezekiel		13:13	46/47
34:4	52/53		50/51
	54/55		
		2 Corinthians	
Daniel		4:7	42/43
9:18	44/45	6:5	54/55
		7:1	46/47
Jeremiah		11:29	50/51
9:23	42/43	12:15	48/49
23:3	42/43		
31:20	40/41	*Galatians*	
		4:13	50/51
Matthew			
15:14	50/51	*Ephesians*	
18:20	54/55	4:3	52/53
24:45	40/41		
	42/43	*Colossians*	
		3:13	54/55
Luke			
1:38	40/41	*1 Thessalonians*	
12:42	40/41	5:14	50/51
	42/43		54/55
	54/55		
		Hebrews	
John		4:12	44/45
10:11–14	38/39	5:3	44/45
10:14	38/39	10:32	38/39
10:28	56/57		
21:17	38/39		

Table of
Non-Scriptural References

Column one indicates the source, and column two identifies the page numbers on which the reference appears in Latin and English in this volume.

AELRED OF RIEVAULX		ANSELM	
Iesu 1.3	44/45	OF CANTERBURY	
Inst incl 32	38/39	'Prayer of a Bishop	
Lam D 2	56/57	or Abbot'	38/39
Oner 1.10	52/53		40/41
15.1	48/49		44/45
28:23–24	50/51		50/51
Spec car Ep.5	42/43	AUGUSTINE	
1.29.84	44/45	*Confessions* 2.1	38/39
1.34.100	50/51		
S 1.33 (Adv Dom)	42/43	BENEDICT, SAINT	
S 6.5 (Nat Ben)	42/43	RB Prol.30	42/43
S 8.2 (Nat Ben)	42/43	RB 2.32	50/51
S 32.1 (Pur)	44/45	RB 35.1	54/55
S 56.5 (Fest Ben)	50/51	RB 64.8	44/45
S 82.1–2 (Fest Ben)	44/45		46/47–49
Vita E Prol.	46/47–49		52/53
	52/53	RB 64.15	56/57

RB 71.1   54/55
RB 73.2, 4   56/57

BERNARD OF CLAIRVAUX
S Div 11.3   42/43

CISTERCIAN MISSAL
Prayer '*Infunde*' for General
Chapter   52/53

GILBERT OF HOYLAND
S 6.2   50/51

GREGORY THE GREAT
Dialogues 2.1   50/51

JOHN OF FÉCAMP
'Prayer for Friends'   38/39
                                     44/45
                                     46/47
                                     52/53
                                     56/57

SALVE REGINA   38/39

WALTER DANIEL
Vita Aelredi 27   48/49

WILLIAM OF SAINT THIERRY
Med 3.3   48/49